P9-DEP-630

Startup Opportunities

KNOW WHEN TO QUIT YOUR DAY JOB

Second Edition

Sean Wise and Brad Feld

Cover images: Memo with paper clip © t_kimura/Getty Images;
background © Nicolas Balcazar/EyeEm/Getty Images
Cover design: Wiley

Copyright © 2017 by Sean Wise and Brad Feld. All rights reserved.

Published by John Wiley & Sons, Inc., Hoboken, New Jersey.

The first edition of *Startup Opportunities* was published by FG Press in 2015.

Published simultaneously in Canada.

No part of this publication may be reproduced, stored in a retrieval system, or transmitted
in any form or by any means, electronic, mechanical, photocopying, recording, scanning,
or otherwise, except as permitted under Section 107 or 108 of the 1976 United States
Copyright Act, without either the prior written permission of the Publisher, or authorization
through payment of the appropriate per-copy fee to the Copyright Clearance Center, Inc.,
222 Rosewood Drive, Danvers, MA 01923, (978) 750-8400, fax (978) 646-8600, or on the Web
at www.copyright.com. Requests to the Publisher for permission should be addressed to the
Permissions Department, John Wiley & Sons, Inc., 111 River Street, Hoboken, NJ 07030,
(201) 748-6011, fax (201) 748-6008, or online at http://www.wiley.com/go/permissions.

Limit of Liability/Disclaimer of Warranty: While the publisher and author have used their
best efforts in preparing this book, they make no representations or warranties with respect
to the accuracy or completeness of the contents of this book and specifically disclaim any
implied warranties of merchantability or fitness for a particular purpose. No warranty may
be created or extended by sales representatives or written sales materials. The advice and
strategies contained herein may not be suitable for your situation. You should consult with a
professional where appropriate. Neither the publisher nor author shall be liable for any loss
of profit or any other commercial damages, including but not limited to special, incidental,
consequential, or other damages.

For general information on our other products and services or for technical support, please
contact our Customer Care Department within the United States at (800) 762-2974, outside
the United States at (317) 572-3993 or fax (317) 572-4002.

Wiley publishes in a variety of print and electronic formats and by print-on-demand. Some
material included with standard print versions of this book may not be included in e-books or
in print-on-demand. If this book refers to media such as a CD or DVD that is not included in
the version you purchased, you may download this material at http://booksupport.wiley.com.
For more information about Wiley products, visit www.wiley.com.

Library of Congress Cataloging-in-Publication Data:

Names: Feld, Brad, author. | Wise, Sean, 1970- author.
Title: Startup opportunities: know when to quit your day job/Brad Feld and
   Sean Wise.
Description: Hoboken, New Jersey: John Wiley & Sons, 2017. | Includes
   index.
Identifiers: LCCN 2017011359 (print) | LCCN 2017009358 (ebook) | ISBN
   978-1-119-37818-1 (cloth) | ISBN 978-1-119-37817-4 (ePDF) | ISBN
   9781-1-19-37819-8 (ePub)
Subjects: LCSH: New business enterprises. | Entrepreneurship.
Classification: LCC HD62.5.F445 2017 (ebook) | LCC HD62.5 (print) | DDC
   658.1/1—dc23
LC record available at https://lccn.loc.gov/2017011359

Printed in the United States of America

10 9 8 7 6 5 4 3 2 1

To Amy and Marisa,
our wives, who are by far the best opportunities we have ever invested in

Contents

Foreword

"Dear Chris. I have an idea that will revolutionize a $34 billion industry . . ."

Do you know what that is? An email I will never open. No matter how elegant the prose that follows, I see a snippet like that in Gmail and immediately hit ARCHIVE.

Why? As you've heard me say for years, "Ideas are cheap. Execution is everything."

At some point, each of us has had that moment where we say, "Wouldn't it be cool if . . . ?" Every single human being is capable of churning those out. In fact, I am certain some of you once thought, "Wouldn't it be cool if I could push a button and have a car and driver show up?" "Wouldn't it be cool if people could rent out their houses for just a couple days at a time?" "Wouldn't it be cool if there were an API for payments?" "Wouldn't it be cool if you could make phone calls and text into your app by using just a little bit of HTML?"

You came up with those ideas, so why aren't you a billionaire founder on the cover of a magazine? You even bought the endearingly vowel-free domain name, so why aren't you going public?

Because all the value, all the magic, all the accomplishment, and everything else that matters in entrepreneurship comes in the grueling months and years following the "Wouldn't it be cool if . . . ?" question.

Since I started making seed investments in 2007, I have been obsessively focused on founders. I spend tons of time with them and go deep in the areas I know well. I never worked on Wall Street or at P&G, and I suck at Excel. So, if we team up, I'm not your supply chain manager or ads optimizer, nor will you catch me estimating Q3 sales five years out.

If we work together, I am there to help you make your product easy and real.

Back in the day, it was expensive to start building a company. Software was proprietary, founders had to buy pricey servers, and they even had to run their own equipment racks in a speedy data center. All of this meant entrepreneurs needed to raise lots of money before they could build anything.

The result? Ideas were splayed across 60-page business plans written by investment banking trainees. Aspiring CEOs were forced to run the investor gauntlet and have every assumption questioned. Hand-wavey bullshit artists with dog-eared copies of *Getting to Yes* and *Starting with No* on their genuine faux leather coffee tables drove the painstakingly Socratic process.

Today, with open source, AWS, GitHub, and coffee shops with free Wi-Fi, there are few barriers to taking an impulse and slapping some code on it. Just $99 will get you a solid logo and smooth-looking homepage that makes it look like you know what you're doing. No more professional networking connections needed, no fancy B-school degrees, and no slick-talking pitch doctors. These days, builders gonna build.

Raise a glass to the democratization of it all! And best of luck to all the now unnecessary investment bankers with incredible PowerPoint and personal grooming skills who have since moved back to New York City to apply their talents to some predatory lending scheme or mass layoff.

But the downside? Too many of you who are founding stuff are skipping the part where smart people beat the shit out of your idea over and over again before anything gets built.

When I first got into this investing business full-time, I was holed up at Brickhouse on Brannon in San Francisco hearing back-to-back pitches. Small teams who could show me live code were impressive. I loved being able to play with a site or an app rather than merely considering a hypothetical.

Yet, almost everything they showed me was irretrievably misguided from the get-go. I met hundreds of entrepreneurs who didn't even know their own competitive landscape, let alone have the ability to describe to me in plain English why they would win the space.

It was devastatingly clear: They hadn't done the intellectual work that would be the foundation for everything that came next.

In 2008, I'd had enough of these frustrating conversations, so my wife and I moved to Truckee, a small mountain town near Lake Tahoe. Our thesis was that instead of running from coffee to coffee, we'd identify the most intriguing minds in startups and invite them up to our house for weekends. We would go deep with the founders whose thinking challenged ours. Whether we were skiing, hiking, cooking, playing music, or snowshoeing, we were also spending that time batting around visions and predictions and controversial points of view. We would sit around for hours in our hot tub, which soon became known as the "jam tub." For days at a time, we just jammed on ideas, pushing one another's reasoning, testing assumptions, and forging moments of clarity and inspiration.

We soon realized that this worked elsewhere as well. Whether we were in Austin, San Francisco, Montana, New York, Paris, Oxford, Boulder, or Vancouver, making time for meaningful group discussion was not only the most fulfilling way to spend time, but it was leading to more genuine friendships and, ultimately, much better ideas across the board.

So who was in those jam sessions? Founders from Twitter, Instagram, Twilio, Uber, Lookout, Stripe—you get the picture. Sure they are legendary companies today, but consider what those early jams were like. For example, as obvious as Uber may seem today, extensive creativity, original thinking, and robust debate were necessary to hone in on the real problems in the industry and focus a solution to build.

These great entrepreneurs didn't just come up with a great idea. They started with a notion and bounced it around a lot before ever starting up the business. Who they bounced it around with was vital. Early co-founders, advisors, friends, and mentors made a huge difference. What they did with the idea mattered. If they just sat on it, it died. But if they ran around and talked to a bunch of prospective customers or users, it got better. If they actively listened to feedback and incorporated some into their plans, it got even better.

The most successful founders are listeners, thinkers, and tinkerers. They are iterative, reflective, and rigorous. They passionately believe they are right but enjoy when their assertions or conclusions are shredded. The very best feel that yes is boring, and they thrive when wrestling with no.

So take that cute, naive idea of yours and throw it to the wolves. Let your friends slap it around. Ask your peers to tear it up. Meet with fellow entrepreneurs and invite them to bury it. Take what's left after your mentors spit it out and head back to the whiteboard. Stay up all night jamming. Do this again and again and again, and you'll realize why founders of billion-dollar companies may be lucky, but their success is never an accident.

I hope to see your name among theirs soon.

Chris Sacca
Montana
March 2017

Preface

Entrepreneurs dream of the magical moment in the creative process when they have a flash of clarity about how to solve a problem or make an innovative product. They often have an interesting story about this moment, and the origin stories of some successful companies have become legend. Yet, this moment of clarity often obscures the massive amount of work required to go from an idea to a real startup. From the outside looking in, a great company appeared out of nowhere. But the entrepreneur knows differently and remembers what had to happen to get from the idea to even the most embryonic startup.

As investors, we hear a simple question from entrepreneurs multiple times a day: "What do you think of my idea?" Sometimes the idea is well formed; often it is vague. Some have already been prototyped, others are just a few sentences in an email. Some have been thoroughly researched by an entrepreneur with deep domain knowledge, others are something completely new and different that the entrepreneur is exploring.

While it is easy to have an idea, it is incredibly hard to translate that idea into a successful business. The startup phase of a company requires a wide variety of activities to go from idea to successful startup. In the past few years, many books have been written about this process, including foundational ones such as *The Lean Startup* by Eric Ries, *The Startup Owner's Manual* by Steve Blank, and *Disciplined Entrepreneurship* by Bill Aulet.

Nevertheless, we continue to hear some version of the same question over and over from aspiring entrepreneurs: "Is my idea any good?" Sometimes it's phrased as "How do I know if my idea is good?" or "When I have an idea, how do I know if it's good?" Often, this morphs into "I have the following three ideas. Which is the best one?"

Many of these entrepreneurs aren't ready to stop what they are doing and dive all the way in to chase their new idea. Some have full-time jobs and are trying to figure out how this entrepreneurship thing works. Others are playing around with multiple ideas at the same time and trying to pick one or are stuck in the ideation phase, coming up with ideas and looking for external validation, but are unwilling to commit to working on a specific idea yet.

Ultimately, they are asking some form of the question "Will there be enough demand for this product that people will use it and pay for it?" Even after being pointed at books and approaches like the Lean Startup, they still have questions about whether their idea is any good.

It's not a simple question to answer. Most successful companies go on a long and winding journey to find the answer. A founder used to write a comprehensive and tightly structured business plan that evaluated all aspects of the potential business. This document took hundreds of hours to write and tried to set up the theoretical case for the business without testing anything.

While business planning isn't obsolete, the business plan is. It has been replaced by methodologies such as the Business Model Canvas, Business Model Generation, Lean Startup, Lean Launchpad, and Disciplined Entrepreneurship. Each of these methodologies uses a structured, experimental approach with quantitative feedback loops from potential users, customers, and partners to evolve an idea to a foundation upon which a startup can be built.

But that still leaves us with the questions "Is the idea any good?" and "Should I pursue this idea?"

It is possible to get to a better starting point if you spend some time in the opportunity evaluation phase. Before you even begin testing the idea and building on it, there are some fundamental questions you can answer. Through our work at Techstars, *Dragons' Den*, and as early stage investors, we have found ourselves asking entrepreneurs the same set of questions repeatedly. While many of our conversations were short and detailed answers often weren't forthcoming, we found that even the simple act of being asked the questions often helped the entrepreneur improve the idea.

   It is not enough that you think your idea is a good idea. Others need to agree with you so that they will work with you either as partners, employees, investors, advisors, or customers. However, many entrepreneurs are afraid to share their idea with others for fear that it might be stolen. But as you'll see in a moment, ideas need oxygen. In addition to engaging supporters and getting feedback, opening up ideas up and sharing them with trusted advisors as you are having the ideas can help evolve these ideas into something that you can build upon to create a startup.

   Our goal with this book isn't to replace existing methodologies. Instead, we want to complement them by giving you a context and a set of tools to help you evaluate your idea before you start putting any meaningful energy into it. Think of this exercise as the precursor to the Lean Startup or the Lean LaunchPad methodologies. We want this to be the book you read before diving into one of these methodologies, especially if you are a first-time entrepreneur.

   The audience for this book isn't just existing entrepreneurs or investors but a much larger class of readers—those who have yet to quit their jobs and take the leap into entrepreneurship. Hopefully, we will help you pick a better idea to build a startup around.

Trust Me, Your Idea Is Worthless

by Tim Ferriss[1]

Earth-shattering and world-changing ideas are a dime a dozen. In fact, that's being too generous.

I've had hundreds of would-be entrepreneurs contact me with great news: They have the next big thing, but they can't risk telling me (or anyone else) about it until I sign some form of idea insurance, usually a nondisclosure agreement (NDA). Like every other sensible investor on the planet, I decline the request to sign the NDA, forgoing the idea, often to the shock, awe, and dismay of the stunned entrepreneur.

Why do I avoid this conversation? Because entrepreneurs who behave this way clearly overvalue ideas and therefore, almost by definition, undervalue execution. Brainstorming is a risk-free, carefree activity. Entrepreneurship in the literal sense of "undertaking" is not. Strap on your seat belt if you're signing up for a startup. It's a high-velocity experience.

If you have a brilliant idea, it's safe to assume that a few very smart people are working on the same thing, or are working on a different approach to solving the same problem. Just look at the number of different travel apps on your iPhone or the number of diet and exercise sites on the web for an example of this.

Overvaluing the idea is a red flag, particularly in the absence of tangible progress. Sure, I miss out on investing in some truly great ideas with this attitude, but that's okay with me; I don't invest in ideas. Nor does Warren Buffett. I'll lose less money than those who do. I can largely control my downside by investing in good people who, even if they fail this go-round, will learn from mistakes and have other fundable ideas (ideas I'll likely have access to as an early supporter). I do not have this advantage when investing in ideas.

One popular startup dictum worth remembering is "One can steal ideas, but no one can steal execution or passion." Put in another light: There is no market for ideas. Think about it for a second: Have you tried selling an idea lately? Where would you go to sell it? Who would buy it? When there is no market, it is usually a very sure sign that there is no value.

Almost anyone can (and has!) come up with a great idea, but only a skilled entrepreneur can execute it. Skilled in this case doesn't mean experienced; it means flexible and action-oriented, someone who recognizes that mistakes can often be corrected, but time lost postponing a decision is lost forever. Ideas, however necessary, are not sufficient. They are just an entry ticket to play the game.

Don't shelter and protect your startup concept like it's a nest egg. If it's truly your only viable idea, you won't have the creativity to adapt when needed (and it will be needed often) in negotiation or responding to competitors and customers. In this case, it's better to call it quits before you start.

Your idea is probably being worked on by people just as smart as you are.

Focus on where most people balk and delay: exposing it to the real world. If you're cut out for the ride, this is also where all the rewards and excitement live, right alongside the 800-pound gorillas and cliffside paths. That's the fun of it.

David didn't beat Goliath with a whiteboard. Go get among it, and prepare to bob and weave.

Note

1. Brad Feld and David Cohen, *Do More Faster: Techstars Lessons to Accelerate Your Startup* (Hoboken, NJ: John Wiley & Sons, 2010), pp. 3–5.

What Is a Startup?

The word *startup* has become an increasing part of the popular lexicon in the past few years. While it has been around for a while, it has recently become ubiquitous for those discussing entrepreneurship and new company creation. But not all new companies are startups.

There is a big difference between two types of entrepreneurial endeavors: (1) local businesses, also called SMEs (small- and medium-sized enterprises) or lifestyle businesses; and (2) high-growth companies, often referred to as *startups* or *gazelles*,[1] a term first used by David Birch in 1979 and refined in 1994 to refer to companies with a minimum of $1 million of revenue that were at least doubling in size every four years.

Local businesses are what they sound like. These are the businesses that you find in your city whose customers are close to the business, such as the corner grocery, local bookstore, nonchain restaurant, or locally owned gas station. Occasionally these local businesses start to expand and turn into multigeography businesses, resulting in a large enterprise, but many are local businesses for the duration of their existence.

In contrast, high-growth companies rarely have a local focus. While they are often started in one location, and, at inception, usually only have a few people involved, the founders of these companies aspire to grow quickly, independent of geographic boundaries. Their customers are all over the world, and regardless of whether the company ever expands geographically, the business is rarely constrained by geography.

In the United States, until recently, all startups were referred to as small businesses. This is a historical artifact of the U.S. Small

3

Business Administration, commonly referred to as the SBA. Until 2010, the U.S. government didn't differentiate between types of entrepreneurial businesses. Thus, the SBA was helpful to some companies but useless to many others, especially the high-growth ones. Government at all levels (federal, state, and local) didn't understand the potential impact of startups as a separate class of company, so all small businesses were lumped together.

In 2010, President Barack Obama announced Startup America[2] and thus the word *startup* catapulted to the forefront of everyone's mind. Through the support of the Case Foundation and the Kauffman Foundation, the Startup America Partnership was launched. This was a private partnership that executed a three-year plan, chaired by Steve Case (the founder of AOL) and led by Scott Case (unrelated to Steve), to define, support, and spread the message of startups throughout the United States.

Today, a startup is recognized as something distinct from a small business. For the definition of startup, we turn to the czar of customer development and grandfather of the Lean Startup movement, Steve Blank, who has coined what we think is the best definition for the term: A startup is a temporary organization formed to search for a repeatable and scalable business model.[3]

Let's break down Steve's definition and explore the different parts:

> A *temporary organization:* A startup does not last as a startup. It either goes out of business or succeeds in finding a solution that customers are willing to pay for.
>
> *To search:* The goal of a startup is to explore, test, and validate an unmet need. This definition recognizes that the startup lifecycle is finite.
>
> *Repeatable and scalable business model:* Initially, all startups are based on assumptions, with the goal of iterating until the assumptions have been validated. Once the business model has been proven and the startup is self-sustainable, it is no longer a startup.

Steve says this in another delightful way: "A startup is not a smaller version of a large company."[4] Instead, a startup is a series of experiments in search of a scalable business.

How to Use This Book

Our goal with this book is to help you figure out in advance which ideas are worth experimenting with. While this book is intended to be read from beginning to end, we have organized it so that you can read each chapter independently. We want to provide you with a structure to evaluate the idea you have in a formal and comprehensive way while allowing you to quickly think about the key issues that will come up.

We aren't trying to create a new methodology for starting a company, nor are we trying to replace approaches like Lean Startup. Instead, we are taking a step back and engaging earlier in the process. This book is intended to be read before you read *The Lean Startup* or participate in a Lean LaunchPad process. We'll provide plenty of context around different approaches and resources for getting your business off the ground, but our primary focus is in helping you with the prestartup, or the opportunity evaluation phase, when you are still deciding whether to put energy into the startup.

In addition to our perspectives, we've included examples from entrepreneurs and the investors who funded them at very early stages. Many of the examples are of companies that have grown substantially. By going back to a point in time near their inception, you can get a sense of how and why the entrepreneur and the investor decided to pursue the opportunity. Other sidebars include expert analysis from practitioners or academics of some of the more important elements in the opportunity evaluation process.

Our primary professional focus is in investing in high-growth startups. Brad's experience, through Techstars and Foundry Group, is primarily in high-tech companies. Sean's experience, through *Dragons' Den* (Canada's version of *Shark Tank*) and his own investing, is primarily in consumer products. To make this book applicable for anyone interested in starting a company, we've used examples from each of these domains.

Who This Book Is For

We wrote this book with first-time entrepreneurs in mind. However, we have received feedback from experienced entrepreneurs that this book has been helpful to them while thinking through their next opportunity.

As entrepreneurship engages a wider range of younger people in our society, we see a dramatic increase in entrepreneurial activities from high school and college students. This book is aimed at them and is intended to be used as a part of an entrepreneurship curriculum.

This book is for educators, particularly those teaching entrepreneurship and opportunity recognition and evaluation courses. If you are a teacher whose students often ask, "How do I know if my idea is worth pursuing?" then this book is for you.

This book is also for friends and family who support the entrepreneur on her complicated and challenging journey. If you are an entrepreneur, you can use it as a source of dialogue with your spouse, your siblings, your parents, and your children.[5]

This book is for fans of *Dragons' Den* and *Shark Tank*. If you have wondered how the judges choose which companies to fund, you'll enjoy this book.

This book is also for investors, especially angel and early-stage investors, as they try to better understand a new business. In the same way that the entrepreneur can use this book to help shape an opportunity, an investor can also use these concepts to help evaluate an opportunity.

Most of all, the book is for all those who have a passion for entrepreneurship, especially those of you who know that only the very best opportunities deserve your blood, sweat, and tears. Ideas may be worthless, but your time, energy, and focus are not. Friends only let friends work on great opportunities.

Notes

1. John Case, "The Gazelle Theory," *Inc.*, May 15, 2001, http://www.inc.com/magazine/20010515/22613.html.
2. The White House's Startup America homepage, https://obamawhitehouse.archives.gov/economy/business/startup-america.
3. Steve Blank, "What's a Startup? First Principles," Steve Blank's blog, January 25, 2010, http://steveblank.com/2010/01/25/whats-a-startup-first-principles/.
4. Steve Blank, "A Startup Is Not a Smaller Version of a Large Company," Steve Blank's blog, January 25, 2010, https://steveblank.com/2010/01/14/a-startup-is-not-a-smaller-version-of-a-large-company/.
5. Don't forget your pets, especially if you have a rubber duck. For more perspective on the value of talking out loud to yourself, see http://en.wikipedia.org/wiki/Rubber_duck_debuggin.

2

The Democratization of Startups

Now is an amazing time to be an entrepreneur. Startup communities are being built all over the world. You don't need significant capital to start a new business. Knowledge about how to start and scale companies is more prevalent than ever.

Twenty years ago, the Internet was starting to be used in a commercial way. Today, an entire generation has grown up net native, and people are living their lives online and unaware of a time when the world wasn't interconnected by technology. The rapid change and increased availability of technology has radically impacted how companies are started and built. The dynamics around barriers to entry, especially in businesses that have constraints around communication and distribution, have shifted in favor of startups.

This applies no matter where you are located—from Silicon Valley to Berlin, from New York City to Iowa City. The emergence of concepts like the sharing economy, the growth of smartphone use and the accompanying app explosion, and the interconnectedness of many business functions are democratizing the ability to start a new company.

The Cost to Launch Is Approaching Zero

In the dot-com boom (1996–2001) software companies needed several million dollars of funding to buy equipment just to get started. There was no Google to help attract users, there was no PayPal to make payments frictionless, there was no AWS (Amazon Web Services) to remotely host your application, and there was no Shopify to build your e-commerce store. Just as it was with the early settlers

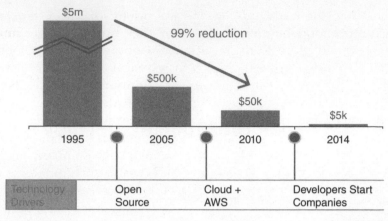

Figure 2.1   Falling Cost of Tech Entrepreneurs Launching Product

in Alaska, there was no infrastructure to support nascent entrepreneurs. If you wanted to launch a jewelry business online in 1996,
you not only had to have kickass jewelry, you had to build your own
storefront and your own payment transaction engine, and you had
to attract customers one at a time. Basically, you had to put all the
pieces together yourself.

By the Web 2.0 era (2007), the cost to start an online business
had dropped to less than $500,000. Much of the infrastructure that
you needed existed in some form. By 2012, cloud computing had
emerged along with software that integrated most of the supply and
demand chains. Now you could get going with under $50,000. Today,
that number is even lower, with the requirement often being a lap-
top, access to free Wi-Fi at a Starbucks, and a few online services.

This radical drop in cost is a result of the rise of Internet infrastructure connecting all aspects of business along with the immi-
gration of billions of people onto the Internet. Upfront Ventures
summarizes this beautifully in the visual representation in Figure 2.1.

The World Is Flat

In 2005, when Thomas Friedman wrote *The World Is Flat*, the meta-
phor of viewing the world as a level playing field set a great backdrop
to what happened around entrepreneurship over the next decade.

Suddenly, due to technology and the broad spread of information, entrepreneurs became geo-agnostic (i.e., they no longer must live in a certain place to do business). As broadband and mobile Internet expanded around the world, physical location mattered much less. Today, you can take care of just about everything your business needs from your smartphone or a browser. You can sell to customers anywhere in the world from anywhere in the world. A one-person operation with a website and a presence on social media can reach consumers across the world as easily as a large company. While mass markets are more available, the ability to use demographic and social media data to identify small, specific, specialized markets has never been greater—or easier.

The Path Is Known

When we studied entrepreneurship in the 1980s, before *entrepreneurship* was a popular word, we were given a book—*The Autobiography of Benjamin Franklin* or *Iacocca: An Autobiography*—and told to glean ideas from their best practices. Maybe we got lucky and stumbled across a copy of Jeffry Timmons' *New Venture Creation: Entrepreneurship for the 21st Century*.

Times have changed. Today, we have several decades of experience studying, discussing, documenting, and formalizing ways startups are created. Instead of an ad hoc, random, or apprentice-based approach, we now have a scientific approach to creating startups. While there are different styles, the most common, now referred to as the Lean Startup approach, was created and popularized by Steve Blank through his theory of Customer Development and his student Eric Ries with his omnipresent book, *The Lean Startup*.

This path has at its core the idea of customer collaboration, which sees founders working with early adopters to shape a product or service that resonates with the customer segment. It is not a new idea, building on the concept of lean manufacturing and the notion of user-driven innovation by MIT professor Eric von Hippel.

The Lean Startup, and methodologies like it, gives us a formalized road map to go from an idea to a startup. It changes the approach from one of overplanning to one of iterative planning in conjunction with feedback from users. Instead of building things in secret, founders are instructed to go to market early with a minimally viable product, test it with users, and then iterate continuously.

Access to Capital

While the cost of getting started has dropped dramatically, access to capital has increased equally significantly. A founder with an idea for a new business but no money had to go hat-in-hand to those with capital, begging and pleading for an investment. The process, including presentations, exhaustive explanations, and multiple projections, often failed to achieve the sought-after funding.

Today, a person starting a new business has access to individual high net worth investors, angel investors, and venture capital funds created for the sole purpose of investing in new ideas and new companies. Accelerator programs, which provide a small amount of capital and a lot of mentoring, help founders hone their early ideas and get positioned to raise additional capital. Online crowdfunding resources, such as AngelList, create an entirely new pool of capital for founders to access.

While founders still must prove the merit of their ideas, their options for funding are greater and the process is generally less convoluted. Furthermore, the balance between the investor and the entrepreneur has shifted. Rather than being dependent on raising

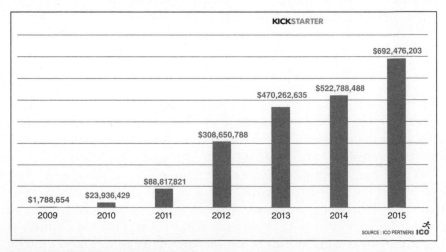

Figure 2.2   Total Amount Pledged per Year

capital to get into the market with a product, you can now quickly get into the market and demonstrate customer demand, which results in an easier path to financing.

The extreme example of this is product crowdfunding, where you no longer need investors to bless your idea. Instead, you can get traction and early revenue before you even build the solution. In 2015, more than $692 million was committed over Kickstarter (the world's leading crowdfunding platform) to products that were not built yet (see Figure 2.2).

With these positives comes a downside. More people than ever are starting companies. The lack of barriers to entry allows terrible ideas to be pursued. Investing time at the very beginning to understand how to come up with a good opportunity is more important than ever.

That is the purpose of this book.

CHAPTER 3

Opportunities

At some point in your life you had an entrepreneurial epiphany. You suddenly came up with an idea that you couldn't stop thinking about. You might have believed it was an idea that could change the world and bring you fame and fortune. It might be something that you wanted to create to solve a problem you had, or it could have been something you were completely fascinated by and obsessed with.

Throughout history, whenever there is a problem or an unmet need, humans have tried to create something to provide a solution. The academic literature talks about these unmet needs as being the result of "suboptimal solutions," a status quo that leaves the user or customer unsatisfied. The telegraph was invented to address the fact that the postal service was a suboptimal solution for rapid communication and addressed the unmet need of instant communication over large distances. Airplanes provided a solution to suboptimal long voyages by ship. Facebook aggregated and improved on several different suboptimal solutions for sharing information with your friends and family.

The Four Criteria for an Opportunity

All opportunities start with an idea. While ideas are at the heart of all opportunities, for an idea to be an opportunity, it must be actionable (i.e., an idea that can't be executed isn't an opportunity) and have the following characteristics:[1]

1. *The idea is durable:* It is not a fad and will last long enough to allow it to be monetized.
2. *The idea is timely:* The market is ready to buy the solution.

3. *The idea is attractive:* The potential rewards and returns on investment far exceed the foreseeable costs and resources to create the product.

4. *The idea adds value:* It must lead to a product or service that creates or adds value for its buyer or end user.

Sean has spent years listening to pitches from entrepreneurs seeking investment on the business reality show *Dragons' Den,* the Canadian version of *Shark Tank.* Throughout this book we'll include short examples from *Dragons' Den* and *Shark Tank* to illustrate our points. We will start with DJ R Dub,[2] an entrepreneur with an idea that missed on all four of these characteristics. DJ R Dub came on *Shark Tank* to raise capital for his "love song dedication show." It didn't go well. The investors declined to fund this entrepreneur because the idea was not:

Durable: The audience/market for radio talk shows is shrinking.

Timely: The golden age of radio is long over, having been cannibalized by iTunes, online streaming services, and other music apps.

Attractive: Running ads against content requires a huge audience and this audience has migrated away from the radio.

Valuable: The founder was focused on a young audience, yet this demographic gets its music from places other than the radio.

What Is Opportunity Evaluation?

While opportunities are often obvious in hindsight, it's hard to evaluate an opportunity when the idea first comes up. The moment the idea occurs to an entrepreneur, it's rarely obvious that the opportunity will be a significant one. This can be because the market is unknown, the technology is nonexistent, or the idea is radical compared to the currently available solutions.

Since your time, energy, bandwidth, and capital are scarce, it is useful to differentiate good from bad opportunities regardless of the role you play in the entrepreneurial ecosystem.

- Entrepreneurs should choose which opportunity to pursue.
- Employees need to decide which companies to join.

- Investors should choose which opportunities to fund.
- Customers decide which products to buy.
- Governments and nongovernmental organizations need to decide which opportunities are worthy of public resources.

Opportunity evaluation is the systematic, objective assessment of the potential of an opportunity.[3] We refer to the unit of measure as the *quantum of return*.

The quantum of return can be the amount of money you think you can make from an opportunity. Investors call this return on investment, or ROI. For example, the ROI of a one-year government bond is 3 percent. If you bought $1,000 worth of bonds, you would receive $1,030 at the end of the year for an ROI of $30, or 3 percent. Not very inspiring, but that's because it's a low-risk investment. Another quantum of return is based on the amount of time you spend on the opportunity. This is commonly referred to as opportunity cost of time or return on invested time (ROIT).[4] Humans have an average life expectancy of about 25,000 days. How you spend each day, or how you "invest your time," should factor into the attractiveness of pursuing a specific opportunity.

The concept of return on invested time applies to entrepreneurs as well as the employees of a startup. As your startup grows, you will need to convince people to join your team instead of being part of a company pursuing a different opportunity. If these prospective employees are going to spend years working for you, they need to believe that they will get a better return on invested time than they would working for another company. If your software developer passes up working at Google for $90,000 a year, then she must believe that her time spent at your startup will generate more wealth than she is passing up. Her decision must also take probability into account. Working at Google is nearly guaranteed to pay her $90,000. To lure her to your startup, the wealth potential must be greater after accounting for the risk that your startup will fail.

While it is difficult to determine the probability of success, your qualitative reaction to the notion of expected ROI and ROIT impacts the decision to pursue an opportunity. They are important quantitative measures, enabling you to look back and measure how things went. Recognize that a billion-dollar idea that fails isn't as valuable as a million-dollar idea that succeeds.

What Is the Cost of Poor Opportunity Evaluation?

Per the Global Entrepreneurship Monitor in 2013,[5] 465 million people between the ages of 18 and 64 around the world were actively engaged in early-stage entrepreneurial activities. Consider how many of these people are pursuing poorly thought-out opportunities, resulting in lost time, effort, and money.

There is an endless stream of opportunities around us each day. Some are good and some are not. Many people fixate on the opportunities missed. Over the years, we've continually heard statements like "XYZ is a great business. I had the idea for XYZ years earlier." These statements are often followed by the speaker rambling on about how wealthy she would be if she had pursued the idea for XYZ.

But the value of the opportunity is often only apparent in hindsight. While the entrepreneur may come up with the idea, if no action is taken, the statement "I had the idea for XYZ years earlier" is irrelevant. Ideas without execution are worth very little. For example, Mark Zuckerberg was not the first person to explore or build a social networking product and company. But, once it became a success, many people wanted to take credit for coming up with the idea, and by extension, the business. The famous quote from the movie *The Social Network*—where Mark Zuckerberg says to the Winklevoss brothers during a deposition, "If you guys were the inventors of Facebook, you'd have invented Facebook"— rings true.

The cost of what could have been created is small when compared to the resources squandered on bad ideas. If an entrepreneur spends all his time, energy, social capital, bandwidth, and money on an idea that turns out to be a poor opportunity, in addition to being out all the time, energy, social capital, bandwidth, and money invested in the poor opportunity, the entrepreneur has a large *opportunity cost*.

Opportunity cost represents "the cost of an alternative that must be forgone to pursue a certain action and the benefits you could have received by taking an alternative action."[6] For example, if an executive decides to go back to school to obtain her MBA, in addition to direct costs (tuition, school books, and bus fare), she will have opportunity costs (salary not earned while in school and work promotions not pursued). To understand the true cost of the MBA, you should account for both direct costs and opportunity costs.

While poor opportunity evaluation has direct costs, the opportunity costs can be more substantial. For every bad idea that moves forward, the resources and direct costs are unavailable for the better ones. Venture capitalists (VCs) invested $29.4 billion in 3,995 deals in 2013, an increase of 7 percent in dollars and a 4 percent increase in deals over the prior year. It is commonly asserted that only 1 percent of companies that pitch VCs get funded. If 3,995 companies got funded, there were hundreds of thousands of companies that pitched VCs that didn't get funding. What's the disconnect? One of the explanations is poor opportunity evaluation by entrepreneurs.

Poor opportunity evaluation isn't limited to VC-backed companies. Of all the businesses that are started each year, a third will be dead within two years and less than half will survive past the five-year mark.[7] Poor opportunity evaluation isn't the sole cause of these failures, but it is a major contributor.

Founder's Perspective: SendGrid
By Isaac Saldana (Co-Founder)

As I've gotten older, I have come to realize what matters most to me when making decisions about how to spend my time. I've found there are four aspects to consider relative to the situation, that make my decision making easier. These aspects are resources, relationships, knowledge, and happiness.

Resources include getting minerals in a video game, more vacation time at a job, oxygen in a workout, or shares in a company. Relationships refer to a network in business, great chemistry and productivity with coworkers, or a great and loving relationship with my wife and kids. Knowledge is powerful because it can't be taken away until death and it can be transferred to the people whom I care about. Finally, happiness, per the documentary *Happy* by Roko Belic, can be achieved by being healthy, experiencing something new, spending time with friends and family, doing some type of play or game, being thankful for what you have, and understanding that you make a difference. If I find a good balance among the four aspects, I can easily move forward with a decision.

Initially, I didn't know SendGrid was a good business opportunity. SendGrid is an email infrastructure service that helps companies deliver transactional email. The data available before I started SendGrid was limited and did not provide good insight into the size of the market or any sign of demand. Email marketing companies existed, but they did not address developers, the main target audience for SendGrid.

I had other potential ideas I could work on that seemed interesting. Unfortunately, the company where I was working at the time was experiencing email

(Continued)

(*Continued*)

deliverability problems and I could not put this problem away. Since I was not an expert on this issue, the more time I worked on it the more interested I became in solving it. Experiencing new problems, learning new protocols and technologies, and solving problems with new approaches kept me going, kept me happy, and kept me learning. Eventually I realized there was the potential for innovation in the email space since I had to solve most of the problems I was experiencing. In this sense, I would be scratching my own itch.

But I still needed validation that an email infrastructure solution could be a real business. Armed with an initial solution, I asked around several Internet forums related to web hosting if anyone was experiencing email deliverability issues and was interested in a solution. To my surprise, a web hosting company replied that it was interested in offering my solution to all its customers. I then approached the two smartest engineers I knew, pitched the idea of an email infrastructure company, and they joined. I was no longer on my own exploring this opportunity. I now had a team.

A few months later, we applied to a startup accelerator called Techstars and got accepted. It is harder to get accepted to Techstars than to Harvard, so this provided validation from the seasoned entrepreneurs, companies, mentors, and investors who are part of the Techstars network. Soon after we went through Techstars, we raised nearly $1 million from Highway 12 Ventures. We later got acquisition offers, but chose instead to grow our business and went on to raise over $20 million from Foundry Group and Bessemer Ventures. Today, we have over 400 employees and millions of dollars in monthly recurring revenue.

I believe there is still much to do in the email space, so SendGrid has a great opportunity in front of it. Understand what matters to you, how you stay excited, and how you can make a difference. Startup opportunities are all around us. Which one will you pick?

Investor's Perspective: SendGrid
By Mark Solon (Techstars, Highway 12 Ventures)

I first met Isaac, Tim, and Jose, the founders of SendGrid, during the second week of the 2009 Techstars Boulder class. I spent 30 minutes with each of the 10 Techstars teams that day and left with a strong positive feeling about SendGrid and its three founders. It was obvious to me in that brief meeting that Isaac was obsessed with solving the problem of large-volume, transactional email deliverability because it had caused him a great deal of frustration in his role at a previous company. I left that first meeting with a feeling that Isaac was on a mission to solve this problem and nothing was going to stop him. Four years later, what stands out in my mind about that meeting was that Isaac and his team could clearly and succinctly articulate the pain point in the market they were going after.

When I returned to Techstars a month later and met with team members again, it was apparent that they were making terrific progress. SendGrid was signing up developers as customers on a regular basis at a low enough price point that they weren't forced to jump through hoops for approval. By keeping the price low (less than $100 per month), SendGrid made it easy for its customers to simply put the service on their credit cards. The company was keen on removing any obstacles for customer adoption and knew it would have an opportunity later to charge for more features and benefits once it had a loyal customer base.

Another thing I observed was that all the other Techstars teams were enamored with Isaac. Many of them went to him for technical help, and they all had great things to say about both the team and the solution. In addition, most of the other teams were already customers of SendGrid. What great validation!

With a month left in the program, I started talking to Isaac on a regular basis. With each conversation, I knew in my gut that he was a very special entrepreneur. I came to believe that, despite his soft-spoken nature, he had an incredibly determined entrepreneur burning inside him. I arrived at Techstars Demo Day with a term sheet to lead the SendGrid seed round.

SendGrid checked three important boxes (team, market, and idea) for me to lead its seed round. Team trumps everything for me at the seed stage. From my perspective, Isaac, Tim, and Jose were serious and credible founders with strong technical chops. Next, they were going after a real pain point in a large and growing market. Finally, their solution worked and wasn't cost prohibitive.

I feel lucky that I've been a small part of SendGrid since its inception. Today, SendGrid has over 100,000 customers, delivers over a billion emails each day, and is regarded as one of the most important cloud infrastructure companies in the world. Opportunities to invest in companies like SendGrid don't come around every day and they're not necessarily easy to spot at the seed stage. While SendGrid had many early signals that it had the potential to become a very large and important company, it was the hard work and great early execution by Isaac, Tim, and Jose that gave the company the chance to be what it is today.

Execution Trumps Opportunity

When Tim Ferriss says, "Trust me, your idea is worthless," he means it. Mary Kay Ash, the founder of Mary Kay Cosmetics, famously stated, "Ideas are a dime a dozen. People who implement them are priceless." In the absence of execution, your idea doesn't go anywhere. Opportunity evaluation helps improve your starting conditions, but you still must execute.

Execution Is What Matters
By Professor Steven A. Gedeon, PhD, MBA, PEng

Entrepreneurship is a fundamental spark of human initiative that enables us to act and shape the world around us. It is about belief in yourself, your ability to create positive change, and your capacity to inspire others to join you in your great adventure. It is about starting with nothing but your own mind and creating dramatic new products and services that didn't previously exist. Entrepreneurship is the most empowering, creative, freedom-loving power in the world.

Entrepreneurship is more than a business discipline. It is a core way of seeing, thinking, and acting that is relevant to all disciplines, faculties, and people. Entrepreneurs don't just see the world as it is, they see it as it can or ought to be and then they make their vision into reality. While entrepreneurs are inventors, planners, thinkers, dreamers, and opportunity spotters, none of these attributes matter if they are not also doers.

Entrepreneurship is about creating value that must be brought forth into existence before it can be exchanged, sold, or used. Even something as abstract as "intellectual property" must be crystallized into a concrete form such as a written document (patent), creative work of art (copyright), or logo (trademark).

Execution is everything. An idea or a business plan has no value on its own. Investors say that they invest in an A team with a B plan over a B team with an A plan. Why? Because business plans are always wrong. Despite all the great analysis and planning, things will go wrong. Sales will take longer, product development will evolve the product into something different than originally envisioned, founders might leave, or a competitor could enter the arena. Often, several of these happen at the same time. Stability for a new company is like stability on a motorcycle. When the motorcycle is stationary or moving slowly, it seems to weigh a ton, easily falls over, and is difficult to get back up again. Yet, at high speeds, its spinning wheels act as gyroscopes to keep you upright. Barriers that seemed insurmountable when you were pushing the bike up a hill become slight bumps in the road when you are traveling fast.

The more quickly you act, the more stable your company becomes and the greater your chance of success. Perfectionists make lousy entrepreneurs. Don't waste time on the perfect business plan as it's probably wrong, anyway. Don't delay speaking to customers, making sales, or launching your product as you wait for the perfect moment. Get out there now!

Initiative, passion, and execution are the only things that you, the entrepreneur, have under your direct control. With that in mind, here are a few specific principles of entrepreneurial execution:

Be an Evangelist: Get out there and talk to everyone who shows interest in your business, including potential customers, suppliers, employees, investors, friends, and peers. Don't keep your idea a secret. Don't disclose your secret sauce, but if your idea or ability to execute is so weak that others can steal it, then let them take it and instead move on to something that you can execute better than anyone else.

Be a Skeptic: Don't just talk. You have two ears and one mouth. Use them in that ratio and listen! Ask hard questions and don't let people get away with telling you what they think you want to hear. Don't just hear the nice things people say. Go deeper and keep asking questions until you find something they don't like or understand. You need to tell people great things about your company, but don't let that blind you to the possibility that your company is not as great as it could be.

Be an Examiner: Set, measure, and track goals. There are more things in a business to keep track of than any single human being can accomplish without a serious project management mind-set. Accordingly, you need to find a way to track the goals that matter and focus your team on achieving them. You need to find a way to translate long-term goals into daily actions. These goals have been referred to as things like key success factors, milestones, OKRs,[8] and targets. You need to make sure everyone on your team is singing from the same songbook.

Tie Rewards to Performance: Align everyone in your organization toward key metrics. Don't just pay people for showing up and looking busy.

Tie Organizational Structure to Strategy: Figure out what your key strategic activities are and put an executive in charge of each one so these activities don't fall through the cracks. Don't just have an organizational structure that gives each founder a VP title with no corresponding key activity. There is no need to use traditional titles like VP Tech or VP Marketing simply due to a lack of imagination or ego inflation on the part of co-founders or early employees. Make sure your executives know which aspects of the business they are responsible for.

Question Your Assumptions and Adapt: Most successful companies make numerous course corrections early in their lives. Since the chance that your original business plan is correct is very low, you should assume from the beginning that you will make major changes to your product, team, and market. As you get out there and present your products and services, you should be learning and changing.

Be a Role Model: You, the entrepreneur, breathe life into the company you create. You instill your values, passion, and work ethic into the company, which creates a company culture through your habits and character. If you show up late, so will your employees. If you can't make and keep commitments, neither will your company. In the early stages of a company, you are the living personification of the character that your company will become. Be a role model for your team to lead a great company.

Risk, Uncertainty, and Ambiguity

Entrepreneurs face many challenges when starting up a new company. Often these challenges are grouped together and collectively referred to as risk, which oversimplifies the situation and often results in a narrow view of what is going on. We like to separate the notion of risk into three different categories: risk, uncertainty, and ambiguity.

Risk occurs when action or inaction may lead to loss, dealing with a future state that may be negative and often can be quantified. In contrast, uncertainty deals with future states that cannot be known and cannot be predicted or quantified. Finally, ambiguity implies knowledge that is unclear. We separate these into three constructs because risks can be mitigated through action, uncertainty is resolved through the passage of time, and ambiguity can be addressed by additional investigation.

While risk takes on many forms, focusing on a few helps clarify what risk is and how to mitigate it. Nobel Prize recipient Herbert Simon suggested the term *bounded rationality* to describe a more realistic conception of the human problem-solving ability. Since humans have finite brainpower and limited time to apply this brainpower, they cannot be expected to solve all difficult problems optimally. Finding the optimal solution often takes more time and resources than would be, well, optimal. You don't drive for 100 miles to get $0.01 off a gallon of gas. You don't visit 10 supermarkets to find the lowest price for every item on your grocery list. Trade-offs should be made and we adopt benchmarks or rules of thumb to help us bound the number of ideas we should explore when deciding.

Cole Egger and James McDonald mitigated market risk with their Sweet Ballz[9] dessert by working with national retailer 7-Eleven to generate $700,000 in sales in the first 90 days. In doing so, they got firsthand market data and validation of their product through sales to end customers. Nathan Jones and Erick Jansen used the crowdfunding site Kickstarter to mitigate market risk for their product, The Freeloader[10], an ultrasleek child carrier that has an integrated frame and a fold-down seat that can hold up to 80 pounds. These two firefighters sold $40,000 in product on Kickstarter before they had even produced it.

Another risk is *management risk*, which asks the question "Is this the best team?" If you are a solo founder, you are the team! While there are cases of solo founders being successful, the odds are against you. Our experience with Techstars has shown that the ideal team size is two to four founders, with at least half of them being focused on the product. If you are a solo founder, one way to mitigate this risk is to find a co-founder.

In contrast to risk, uncertainty is much harder to address. Uncertainty is the absence of specific data or support for a concept that can only be addressed by the passage of time. Rather than ignore uncertainty, there is significant value in articulating it during the opportunity evaluation phase. Clearly stating what the uncertainty is and trying to nail down how long it might take to resolve will help clarify things. If the uncertainty is unbounded and will last forever, that's a real problem. If the uncertainty will be resolved after six months of activity, that's manageable.

Finally, ambiguity can be addressed continually throughout the life of the company. It's particularly useful to focus on this during the opportunity evaluation stage, as clarifying issues and situations that are ambiguous and can be debated helps bring clarity to the opportunity.

The Issue of Bias

Opportunity evaluation is a highly subjective process. Whether you are an entrepreneur or investor, you bring your own history, experience, knowledge, and perspective to the process of evaluating an opportunity. We refer to this as bias. While bias is helpful, it can also be dangerous since it often impacts evaluations significantly and creates blind spots that can be difficult to mitigate. It's important to know and understand your own biases in the context of an opportunity.

KILLER BIAS: PSYCHOLOGICAL TRAPS THAT CATCH ENTREPRENEURS AND INVESTORS
By Professor Dave Valliere, MEng, MBA, PhD, PEng

Every day, everywhere around the world, opportunities are being evaluated and significant resource commitments are being made. Which startups to fund? Which founders to back? These are questions with enormous social and economic consequences. Look around and you'll see these killer biases happening everywhere, including in yourself. If you know them in advance, you can avoid the killer bias trap.

There are all kinds of people who need to know how to spot a great business idea. Some are entrepreneurs trying to decide whether this is the opportunity into which they should put their heart and soul. Some are investors trying to discover the one that will yield returns big enough to offset the other failed investments they've made. Some are potential employees, suppliers, business partners, or intermediaries. Each has a different perspective and different objective for the

(Continued)

(*Continued*)

opportunity evaluation process. But all operate with the same flawed human mind, trying to assess the idea and potentially falling prey to the same common psychological biases—the kinds of traps that catch everyone unless we are fully aware of them and take steps to avoid them. The following are four of the most pervasive psychological biases that often trick both entrepreneurs and their investors into making bad decisions that can kill new ventures and wipe out investments.

Confirmation bias arises whenever we have formed a strongly held opinion or view about something, particularly when we have made a big effort to gather and analyze a lot of information before arriving at our opinion. There are two dangerous effects that may result from confirmation bias. First, you can become attuned and receptive to information that appears to support your opinions. People tend to notice every newspaper article that can be interpreted to support their belief. Investors who have fallen prey to confirmation bias tend to view and accept as true every occurrence in the world that can possibly be an example of the phenomenon in which they believe.

The second dangerous effect of confirmation bias is that you can become blind to information that appears to refute your opinion. Reviewers suffering from confirmation bias often cease to look for information that might contradict their preformed opinion. Furthermore, if the world shoves the conflicting information into their faces, they find some way to rationalize it or deny it. They say, "Yeah, but . . ." and then find some trivial difference that allows them to dismiss the contradictory evidence as an irrelevant special case rather than change their opinions because that would mean admitting being wrong in the first place. It can suddenly seem like confirming cases and examples are everywhere around us, and it can appear that no counter evidence exists. This is an illusion—the rates of occurrence and nonoccurrence have not changed. It is only our awareness and perception that have changed.

Because of this, entrepreneurs and investors should always attempt to remain flexible and open to the possibility that their opinions and assumptions may turn out to be false. Opportunity evaluators should attempt to always remain humble and receptive to the reality that the marketplace will try to teach them. They should make sure they are open to having their assumptions proved wrong.

But it's often not enough if entrepreneurs don't also take active measures to counteract confirmation bias. Investors face the same challenges around confirmation bias and are generally more difficult to coach, especially once they've formed an opinion about whether a market space is hot. Both entrepreneurs and investors need to take deliberate actions to keep confirmation bias in check, such as intentionally seeking contradictory information or contrarian opinions from experts. The real test of whether you have a good business idea is not your ability to find information that says yes, but your inability to find information that says no.

To avoid confirmation bias, spend your time trying to find information that refutes your beliefs instead of more information that supports them.

The next killer bias is *overconfidence*, which is having a belief in one's abilities that is greater than the objective facts warrant. While it is good when entrepreneurs are confident, those who are unable to recognize the limits of their remarkable talent can cause problems. Overconfidence is a particularly hard bias to detect in oneself, since people who are overconfident in their abilities are usually also overconfident in their self-awareness and ability to correct for their own biases. *Overconfidence* is an umbrella term that encompasses a group of related biases, including the planning fallacy or the "90/90 rule" (i.e., the first 90 percent of a project takes the first 90 percent of the budget, and the final 10 percent of the project takes the second 90 percent of the budget), and personal attribution error (i.e., if things go right it's because I'm so smart and skilled, but if things go wrong it's because someone else screwed up). Both are examples of having unreasonably high beliefs in oneself.

Psychometric tests of entrepreneurs and investors repeatedly show some amazingly high levels of overconfidence. This is a cause for concern. These individuals are highly confident and are perfectly right to feel that way since they are highly skilled and capable. In fact, you might argue that confidence is a necessary trait for both entrepreneurs and investors. But, while their abilities might well be 50 percent better than the average person's, they tend to think and act as if their abilities were 500 percent better. For entrepreneurs, this means they often think they can accomplish much more than they can and that their chances of succeeding in a risky venture are much better than they are. The same phenomenon holds for investors, who will be overconfident in their abilities to pick winners and add value to their investments. There's a real lesson in the observation that most VC funds have a hit ratio of only 1 in 10 investments becoming successful. But most VC investors are unable to learn from it because they are caught in their own overconfidence.

To avoid overconfidence bias, make your decisions based on objective data about what you have achieved in the past not what you subjectively think you should be able to do in the future.

The third killer bias is *availability bias*, which is the mistaken belief that situations that are easy for an individual to imagine must be very common out in the world (or the converse—that if you've never personally seen a black swan[11] then they must not exist). While this is seductive reasoning, it is false logic and can be extremely dangerous when generalized. With proper perspective, we can see that our own experience, while a deep and vivid source of insight, is still just a data set with a sample size of one, which is hardly enough to use as the foundation for an entire business strategy. Statisticians will remind us that any sample with fewer than 40 responses will fail to meet even the most basic assumptions of statistical significance. We should guard against this bias by reminding ourselves regularly that the plural of anecdote is not data.

Entrepreneurs who are caught by this bias often exhibit "the market is me" behavior—they believe that if they like the proposed new product, then thousands of other people are going to like it also. This is a weird conclusion,

(Continued)

(Continued)

especially since we celebrate entrepreneurs for being so unlike other people, for thinking and seeing so differently than others, and for being willing to act where other people would not. Therefore, entrepreneurs are often not suitable to use as benchmarks for the marketplace.[12]

The exact same problem occurs on the investors' side of the table. In their case, it often sounds something like "I heard that BigVCFund got a 10× exit in the cloud computing space, so I'm going to invest in the next cloud computing deal that crosses my desk."

To avoid availability bias, keep reminding yourself that your experience is unique and that there is no reason to think that it corresponds to what real market data would say about the average person.

The final bias to be wary of is a phenomenon known as *prospect theory*, which explains three interrelated biases. First, people give too much emotional weight to small chances, thinking that a 1 percent chance is much better than no chance at all and that a 99 percent chance is much worse than a sure thing. The strength of this belief can be witnessed at any lottery ticket kiosk. Second, people treat chances of winning something much differently than they treat the chances of avoiding the loss of something. For example, consider offering the chance of winning at least $250 to entice people to accept a chance of losing $100, regardless of the actual odds. Third, people judge these wins and losses not in absolute terms but relative to where they expected to be or where they told other people that they'd be, which is known as their *anchor point*. These biases combine to create a two-sided irrational phenomenon that catches many people off balance. On the one hand, if we are winning (or even if we are losing but not as badly as we expected to lose), we tend to become overly conservative and reluctant to take sensible or attractive gambles. We try to lock in our wins, thinking that a bird in the hand is worth two in the bush. On the other hand, if we are losing (or even if we are winning, but not as grandly as we told everyone we would), we tend to become reckless risk-takers who throw Hail Mary passes in the slim hope that we can catch up to where we think we ought to be.

This phenomenon is the mechanism that drives escalating commitment, which is when you throw good money after bad in the hopes that the original losses can still be somehow salvaged. This is based on the stubborn human refusal to recognize that sunk costs are always irrelevant when deciding in the present moment. An investor who has watched the value of his investment fall in a clearly doomed startup company will still be strongly biased to participate in any subsequent round of funding in a futile attempt to keep the company alive for a bit longer to avoid having to accept that the first-round money is irretrievably lost.

Prospect theory warns opportunity evaluators that they cannot trust their gut instincts when assessing probabilities of success and that their perceptions will be strongly skewed by recent history. It says that they must ignore the emotional perception that losses hurt more than wins elate and that they must be particularly careful when announcing targets lest they become anchor points that will force them into irrational escalating commitments. Investors may love entrepreneurs who set kick-ass targets and, blinded by their overconfidence, loudly proclaim that these Big Hairy Audacious Goals[13] will be achieved or exceeded. Such acts come with huge risks of becoming trapped in biases that will drive bad decisions and destroy value.

To avoid escalating commitment biases arising from prospect theory, use objective calculations to determine the expected value of uncertain choices and be very careful about the public commitments.

Notes

1. Jeffrey A. Timmons and Stephen Spinelli, *New Venture Creation: Entrepreneurship for the 21st Century* (New York: McGraw-Hill International, 2010).
2. *Shark Tank*: Season 5, Episode 4.
3. J. Michael Haynie, Dean A. Shepherd, and Jeffrey S. McMullen, "An Opportunity for Me? The Role of Resources in Opportunity Evaluation Decisions," *Journal of Management Studies*, 46, no. 3 (2009): 337–361.
4. Razvi Doomun and Nevin Vunka Jungum, "Business Process Modelling, Simulation and Reengineering: Call Centres," *Business Process Management Journal* 14, no. 6 (2008): 838–848.
5. GEM 2013 Global Report, January 20, 2014, www.gemconsortium.org/docs/3106/gem-2013-global-report.
6. MoneyTree Report by PricewaterhouseCoopers LLP and the National Venture Capital Association, based on data from Thomson Reuters, Q4 2013/Full-year 2013, www.pwc.com/en_US/us/technology/assets/pwc-moneytree-q4-and-full-year-2013-summary-report.pdf.
7. SBA Office of Advocacy, Frequently Asked Questions, https://www.sba.gov/sites/default/files/FAQ_Sept_2012.pdf.
8. OKRs are "objectives and key results." For a great video from Rick Klau at Google Ventures on how Google sets goals, see https://www.gv.com/lib/how-google-sets-goals-objectives-and-key-results-okrs.
9. *Shark Tank*: Season 5, Episode 1.
10. *Shark Tank*: Season 5, Episode 3.
11. If you are unfamiliar with black swans, we encourage you to read Nassim Nicholas Taleb's book, *The Black Swan: The Impact of the Highly Probable* (New York: Random House, 2010).
12. There is a big exception, which we've called "scratching your own itch." The story of the founding of SendGrid from earlier in the chapter is a great example of this.
13. Jim Collins, *Built to Last: Successful Habits of Visionary Companies* (New York: HarperCollins, 2002), ch. 5.

4

Approaches to Opportunity Evaluation

There are almost as many approaches to opportunity evaluation as there are opportunities. However, most approaches fall into one of two categories: (1) a stage-gate process or (2) a feedback-loop-based approach involving agile decision making.

A stage-gate process has a series of stages—typically discovery, scoping, building the business case, development, testing, and launch. Between each stage is a "gate" that prompts a review and a decision about whether to go to the next stage, do more evaluation, or kill the project.

The feedback loop process follows a build, measure, and learn approach that is based on the belief that you can only get the information you need by beginning to build what you think your customers want.

The stage-gate process often produces a business plan that asks the question "Is this opportunity worth pursuing?" while the feedback loop process produces something in the form of a business model canvas and asks the question "What assumptions would have to be true for this to be an opportunity worth pursuing?"

Where Does Opportunity Evaluation Fit into the Overall Startup Process?

Most attempts to model the entrepreneurial process include opportunity evaluation as a key stage in the creation of a new venture. The cliché "look before you leap" applies, and evaluating an opportunity before investing time, energy, and money is the best way to do that.

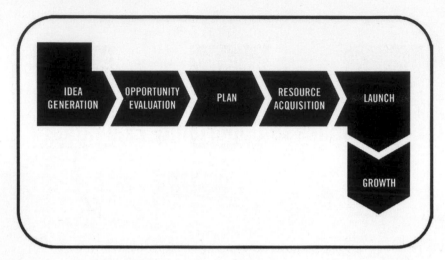

Figure 4.1   Duke Center Entrepreneurial Process Model

The Duke Center for Entrepreneurship and Innovation suggests that the entrepreneurial process (see Figure 4.1) can be broken into distinct phases, namely:

- Idea generation
- Opportunity evaluation
- Plan
- Resource acquisition
- Launch
- Growth

Barringer and Gresock (2008) describe the application of the stage-gate model to opportunity evaluation as shown in Figure 4.2.

Today, many feel that new venture creation follows a much less direct and much more iterative journey such as the one outlined in Eric Ries's Lean Startup model, as shown in Figure 4.3.

The idea of a startup evolving as the result of many repetitive iterations of customer development suggests anything but a linear path to success. Thomas Edison is famous for saying, "I have not failed. I have just found 10,000 ways that don't work." It's no surprise that the phrase "fail faster" is firmly embedded in today's entrepreneurial vernacular.

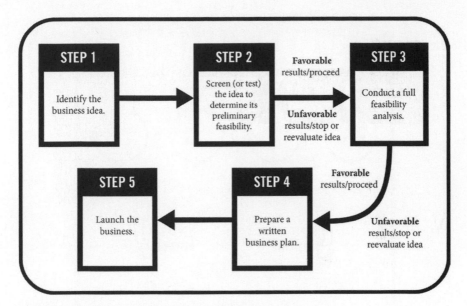

Figure 4.2   Barringer and Gresock (2008) Stage-Gate Model[1]

The evolution of Steve Blank's Customer Development and Alex Osterwalder's Business Model Generation to Eric Ries's Lean Startup continues as more people study, experiment, dissect, and iterate on the startup process. For example, Bill Aulet, head of the Martin Trust Center for MIT Entrepreneurship, published *Disciplined Entrepreneurship*, a new approach building on what has come before but incorporating many lessons learned from companies created and launched at MIT.

Opportunity evaluation can be used in advance of each of these approaches to get more clarity on what to work on before the iterative loop begins. Opportunity evaluation is meant to be a nimble starting point to create focus to apply to a Lean Startup, Lean LaunchPad, or Disciplined Entrepreneurship process.

Overview of Business Model Generation

Osterwalder, with his concept of Business Model Generation, suggests that all business opportunities start by examining the fundamentals of any business model. By defining and exploring nine core elements of a business model, you challenge and investigate the

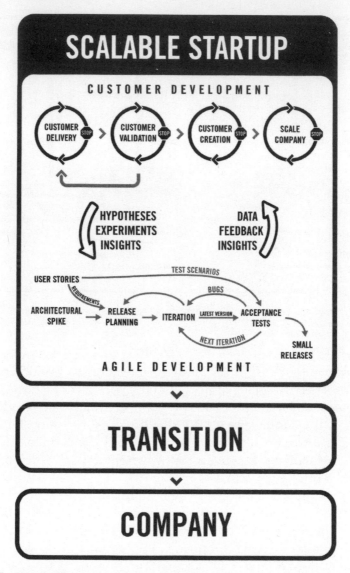

Figure 4.3   Scalable Startup

Adapted from an Eric Ries slide that borrows from J. Donovan Wells's *Extreme Programming*[2]

underpinnings of a potential opportunity, converting the elements into testable hypotheses. The nine components of the Business Model Canvas are Key Partners, Key Activities, Key Resources, Value Propositions, Customer Relationships, Channels, Customer Segments, Cost Structure, and Revenue Streams.

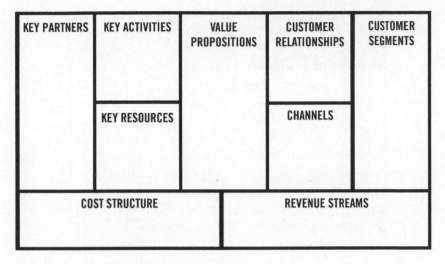

KEY PARTNERS	KEY ACTIVITIES	VALUE PROPOSITIONS	CUSTOMER RELATIONSHIPS	CUSTOMER SEGMENTS
	KEY RESOURCES		CHANNELS	
COST STRUCTURE			REVENUE STREAMS	

Figure 4.4   Osterwalder (2010) Business Model Canvas

The template for the business model canvas is shown in Figure 4.4.

By addressing each of the building blocks shown in Figure 4.4, you begin to identify the assumptions on which your opportunity rests. For example, if you can't articulate the customer segments efficiently, you may have an opportunity with great potential but with no ability to proceed. By adopting the use of the business model canvas, you will explore the obstacles ahead while always keeping the following quote, often erroneously attributed to Machiavelli, in mind: "Entrepreneurs are simply those who understand that there is little difference between obstacle and opportunity and can turn both to their advantage."[3]

Overview of Customer Development and Lean Startup

Sean started working with startups in 1997 while he was with Ernst & Young. His job was to facilitate the success of high-growth ventures. Fresh out of law school, and with only his own entrepreneurial experience to rely on, he immediately began looking for a Rosetta Stone of startups, a magical key that would help him understand why some startups fail while others succeed. Fifteen years later, he found it.

During the summer of 2012, Sean studied under Stanford Professor Steve Blank. The class was on how to teach the Lean LaunchPad approach to students, and it changed how Sean thought about start-ups. Blank's basic tenets can be summarized as:

- No business plan survives first contact with customers.
- Get out of the building to find answers.
- Launch early, launch often.

Blank asserted that spending months writing a business plan and then raising funds in secret to build a product in stealth mode was fundamentally wrong. After his own experience raising a lot of money only to flame out after failing to launch a product that customers bought, Blank tells founders that they should work with customers to refine a crude product into a great product. He favors a more dynamic process, one where founders launch a minimal prototype that does only the one thing that customers need and then tests this product with actual customers.

Using customer feedback allows market demand to validate the founders' efforts. After all, if the pain being mitigated is so great that customers will accept a less than perfect solution, founders could spend their time improving the product, not searching for a market.

This idea of customer development was a radical departure from previous approaches to starting a business. No more spending two years and $2 million on a fully robust solution only to find out that customers don't care.

In Professor Blank's class, Sean learned about the professor's prodigy, Eric Ries, who in 2008 had coined the term *Lean Startup*.[4] Ries integrated Blank's customer development concept with theories and processes from agile development and lean manufacturing. Like Blank, Ries believed in collaborative development. To Ries, *lean* means:

- *Low burn*: Only spend money on the basics. Save the bells and whistles for later.
- *Customer feedback*: Don't fall in love with your hypothesis and assumptions. Don't push products; allow customers to pull them.
- *Rapid prototyping*: Build something quickly, which is referred to as a *minimum viable product* (MVP), and then test it with

customers. Use what you learn to make changes to the prototype and repeat until your crappy prototype becomes an awesome solution.

Ries dubbed this idea *ferocious customer-centric rapid iteration*, and it has gone on to become the foundation of the Lean Startup movement.

Overview of the Disciplined Entrepreneur

After being a multiple-time entrepreneur who got better each time, Bill Aulet returned to his alma mater, MIT, to teach students what he wished he had learned 20 years earlier when he began his first startup. He wanted to create a rigorous yet practical approach where he assembled the best proven tools to increase an entrepreneur's odds of success and then provide a road map for when and how to apply the tools. He codified what he had learned the hard way in his experiences while also working with academics to ensure proper perspective and rigor.

The result is an iterative 24-step process called *Disciplined Entrepreneurship* that helps students progress from "I have an idea/technology/passion" to "I have a product that people are paying me money for." He codified this approach in his book *Disciplined Entrepreneurship: 24 Steps to a Successful Startup.*

The 24 steps in the framework can be categorized into six themes:

1. Who is your customer?
2. What can you do for your customer?
3. How does your customer acquire your product?
4. How do you make money from your product?
5. How do you design and build your product?
6. How do you scale your business?

The process is highly iterative and each step is designed so that as you learn more, you will find reason to go back and revise your work in earlier steps. The framework is designed to help entrepreneurs, particularly first-time entrepreneurs, understand where to start and how to move forward to create a product that customers will want that will result in an economically sustainable new venture.

Disciplined Entrepreneurship can be used for all kinds of new ventures—hardware, software, services, and consumer products—regardless of whether a for-profit or mission-driven model will be used. Startups such as Okta, Lark Technologies, Locu, FINsix, Fast-Cap Systems, WeCyclers, Shop Soko, and Essmart have benefited from this approach.

Disciplined Entrepreneurship has proven valuable because it does not seek to reinvent entrepreneurship but rather to integrate many of the proven techniques that are discussed in individual books and resources.

A Modern Version of the Scientific Method

If you think back to high school science, a lot of this may feel like an entrepreneurial version of the scientific method. Per the *Oxford English Dictionary*, the scientific method is defined as:

> A method or procedure that has characterized natural science since the 17th century, consisting in systematic observation, measurement, and experiment, and the formulation, testing, and modification of hypotheses.

The key words in that definition are: *systematic, measurement,* and *experiment.* Under this discipline, an entrepreneur should no longer rely solely on her gut but should instead systematically observe, test, and measure her assumptions before proceeding. The results of these efforts will help provide the raw material for responses to typical investor questions such as:

- Why offer this solution?
- How do you know your customers want this?
- How did you determine price?

Answer these questions with facts derived from direct customer testing and you stand on solid ground. Answer these questions with anything else and you are on shaky ground. The Lean Startup and the customer development cycle that underlie your exploration provide a systematic, testable, and measurable technique to apply the scientific method to startup development and growth. To use this approach, entrepreneurs should first produce a Lean Canvas (a tool explored in more detail later) filled with testable hypotheses, which are falsifiable claims (claims that can be disproved) that can be objectively tested using the scientific method.[5] Such a hypothesis must be stated in a way that makes it easy to show when it is wrong. The following are some examples:

- I believe that users want to send messages from point A to point B faster than courier, fax, or phone. (email)
- I believe, globally, more people want to access general knowledge than can afford the *Encyclopedia Britannica*. (Wikipedia)
- I believe that people want to send and receive email while away from their desks. (BlackBerry)
- I believe teenagers want to send messages that expire and can't be recorded for later use. (Snapchat)

All of the preceding examples:

- Are assumptions underlying a business model
- Are written down
- Can be proven wrong
- Can be actionable
- Can be tested with customers using an MVP

Eric Ries and Sarah Dillard summarized this on the Harvard Business School blog.[6]

Firms that follow a hypothesis-driven approach to evaluating entrepreneurial opportunity are called *lean startups*.

Entrepreneurs in these startups translate their vision into falsifiable business model hypotheses, then test the hypotheses using a series of MVPs, each of which represents the smallest set of features and activities needed to validate a concept. Based on test feedback, entrepreneurs must then decide whether to persevere with their business model, pivot by changing some model elements, or abandon the startup.

Dan Martell, CEO and founder of Clarity, shows how simple it is to test a hypothesis. Martell tested his initial web-based MVP for Clarity by including a "buy now" button. His hypothesis was that if the service he offered was valuable, users would want to buy it. The buy now button didn't work, but instead led users to a simple landing page that said thank you and acknowledged them for their interest. After the buy now button was clicked thousands of times, Martell knew he had a solution customers wanted. With this proof of concept in hand, he was confident in building out the rest of his solution.[7]

Founder's Perspective: Ubooly
By Carly Gloge (Co-Founder)

Walking down the toy aisle we were amazed at how toys have regressed since our childhood and how the industry is now completely based on brand affiliation rather than value. We started Ubooly with a goal that seemed simple enough—to make a magical stuffed animal powered by your iPhone. Our toy would automatically update with new content over Wi-Fi, which would enable us to pump new value into the product each month.

Like a lot of startups, we charged ahead, naïve to the challenges of distribution and adapting to consumer behavior—possibly the biggest barriers between a great product and success.

Our first test was on Kickstarter, an important step in determining whether there was an audience that cared about what we were building. The initial burst of users that we gained through this campaign provided the critical insight needed to steer us toward a larger opportunity.

I think it is typical for startups to begin with the premise of "This would be awesome!" only to find out later that no one is actively searching for that awesome thing, if for no other reason than it simply hasn't ever existed. The initial product we built was simply a better toy, and we were lucky that our community guided us down a rabbit hole filled with more meaningful aspirations. We received requests from parents asking if Ubooly could teach their kid a new language and discovered that the toy was being used as a therapy tool for kids with autism.

Our customers told us of an itch that could not be scratched by mainstream toys. We realized that a smart toy wasn't the draw. Parents want smart kids. It seems obvious, but we had completely missed the mark in the beginning. This new wisdom has changed the way we think about our business. Knowing the levers that parents respond to when they are thinking about their kids gives us a path to become a billion-dollar brand. Our mission is no longer to deliver a toy that talks and listens but to help grow kids into smarter, more creative, and overall better human beings.

This big opportunity also comes with a big goal. To produce a toy that delivers on all those promises, we'll need kids to play with our toys for a very long time. Therefore, our number one goal is retention. After a year of focusing on keeping kids engaged each day, we now have more than seven times the retention of other toys. A sticky product that delivers on a need that users are searching for—this is a product that can grow organically. It may seem like a slow path to entrepreneurs in the enterprise space, but when competing against consumer products that are powered by astronomically high marketing dollars, growth through your customers can be an amazing foothold. While the big boys are pumping millions into advertising budgets to sell kids on their next toy, the Ubooly community grows and continues to engage with and share a product that it trusts.

This also means that when we release new products and content, we don't need to pay to reacquire our own customers. The average American kid receives 70 new toys each year (a big opportunity), but Mattel spends $700 million annually on marketing to sell just 10 of those toys. To play in this space we can't compete on spend. We've come to realize that real opportunity comes from striking a nerve, not shiny new products. While shiny new products can get you press and possibly funding, soon those folks will move on to the next shiny product. In our case, real opportunity comes from delivering access to education in a format that kids can't put down—concrete value in the eyes of our customers.

Investor's Perspective: Ubooly
By Stephanie Palmeri (SoftTech VC)

To call my investment in Ubooly, a talking stuffed creature, unusual for a VC seems an understatement. At my VC firm, SoftTech VC, we categorize Ubooly within the "new areas" section of our fund, given its unique and potentially disruptive nature. But when you look beneath Ubooly's cute, fuzzy exterior, you find an edutainment company that lies at the intersection of several key investment themes for my firm—including mobility, education, and the Internet of Things— with a strong founding team and a differentiated go-to-market strategy.

Focusing on the market first, we have witnessed a proliferation of smart devices being used at home by children as young as toddlers. When we invested in Ubooly, 30 percent of children played with smartphones, and that number continues to climb. These devices have become a conduit for education and learning. Finally, Ubooly capitalizes on the usage of smart devices to power traditionally inanimate objects.

The most critical element to the success of a startup is its founders: the folks who transform a vision into a company. We believed Ubooly's founding team was uniquely primed to capitalize on this edutainment opportunity. Carly Gloge's experience building startup brands, Isaac Squire's technical expertise, and their combined track record building successful mobile apps through their first business together were strong signals.

Ubooly's Kickstarter preorders also provided a strong indicator of the market opportunity. While founders increasingly leverage crowdfunding and preorder platforms today, Carly and Isaac were early movers on this front. For the Ubooly team, Kickstarter backers helped steer the company toward its emphasis

(Continued)

(*Continued*)

on education. For investors, the Kickstarter campaign not only demonstrated early customer and retailer demand, but also gave us an early indication that international demand was extremely high.

It's not hard to stand out when you pitch a talking orange stuffed animal to investors, but beyond its cute factor, Ubooly offered a unique value proposition to its customers (parents) and its consumers (children). It combined entertainment value for children (a toy children are excited to play with) with educational value for parents (my child is learning as he or she plays). Plenty of gaming apps entertain, but leave children sedentary and parents feeling guilty about screen time. Conversely, retention is a major issue for many education-focused apps—they just aren't fun. Ubooly struck a distinctive balance between a toy children find engaging and a companion parents trust to make their children smarter.

Ubooly's distribution and monetization models also made the company stand out. From the start, Ubooly was primed to take advantage of two unique distribution channels—retail distribution (online at first, offline later) and app store distribution. We believed exposure to Ubooly through multiple channels would help scale the Ubooly brand. Additionally, each channel offered its own revenue stream. Through the combination of physical product and software, Ubooly could monetize through the sales of the plush toy while extending the lifetime value of a customer through in-app purchases of lessons and learning packs.

In just a year since we invested, Ubooly is available on four continents (North America, Europe, Asia, Australia) and speaks five languages (English, Japanese, French, German, Italian). Early-stage companies rarely operate outside the United States at all, let alone have this broad of a geographic reach. Not too shabby for a mobile-powered, cuddly creature from Boulder, Colorado.

Notes

1. Bruce B. Barringer and Amy R. Gresock, "Formalizing the Front-End of the Entrepreneurial Process Using the Stage-Gate Model as a Guide: An Opportunity to Improve Entrepreneurship Education and Practice," *Journal of Small Business and Enterprise Development* 15, no. 2 (2008): 289–303.
2. Eric Ries, "The Lean Startup: Doing More with Less," Gov 2.0 Conference, September 9–10, 2009, http://assets.en.oreilly.com/1/event/30/Lean%20.Startups%20Doing%20More%20with%20Less%20Presentation.pptx.
3. Some people think this is a quote from Machiavelli. But it's not: http://ian chadwick.com/machiavelli/addenda/machiavellian-misquotes/.
4. Eric Ries, "The Lean Startup," *Startup Lessons Learned*, September 2008, updated April 2011, www.startuplessonslearned.com/2008/09/lean-startup .html.

5. Thomas Eisenmann, Eric Ries, and Sarah Dillard, "Hypothesis-Driven Entrepreneurship: The Lean Startup," Harvard Business School Background Note 812-095, December 13, 2011, revised July 2011, www.hbs.edu/faculty/Pages/item.aspx?num=41302.
6. Ibid.
7. *The Naked Entrepreneur* with Professor Sean Wise, March 3, 2013, episode featuring Dan Martell, http://nakedentrepreneur.blog.ryerson.ca/2013/03/03/episode-video-dan-martell/.

CHAPTER 5

People

Sean ran a survey for the accounting firm Ernst & Young a decade ago where he asked startup investors to weigh various elements used in their investment decision process. By far, the most important element was people, weighing in at over 40 percent. It's not surprising to hear investors repeat lines like:

- Bet on the jockey, not the horse.
- An A team with a B idea beats a B team with an A idea.
- People is to opportunity as location is to real estate.

Without people to create the business all you have is an idea. While most of the elements around a business are continuously changing, people are the hardest elements to change and are often the slowest to evolve. Remember that people are complicated.

Team

While investors value serial entrepreneurs, founders who have created more than one company, they love serial management teams. A team of founders who have worked together is a treasure, and a team of founders who have previously built a successful startup is a great treasure. Regardless of experience, a highly functional team generally trumps a solo founder.

At Techstars, we've invested in almost 1,000 companies. While a few of them were solo-founder teams, the vast majority had between two and four founders. We believe that two to four founders is the

43

right number and that at least half of them should be focused on the product. A founding team of four, with three businesspeople and one engineer, is a suboptimal configuration, as the engineer will spend most of his time responding to the businesspeople, and the businesspeople won't have enough to do.

The dynamics among the people on the team are critically important. Some founding teams consist of best friends, while others are composed of people who have met recently. Developing a constructive and effective working relationship is crucial, especially since founders won't agree on everything or have similar styles. Many of the best teams we've worked with have had plenty of conflict, and at Foundry Group, we talk about the importance of "brutal honesty delivered kindly" as part of our culture. The key is not lack of conflict, but figuring out how to work through and resolve the inevitable conflicts.

When investors evaluate a team, they look carefully at how the founders interact with one another. A team that doesn't have conflict may not have what it takes to make the hard decisions. The differences of opinion should be challenging enough to ensure decisions are thoroughly vetted, yet amicable enough to overcome the daily grind of startup life.

Harvard professor Noam Wasserman recently wrote a fantastic book on founding teams. *The Founder's Dilemmas: Anticipating and Avoiding the Pitfalls That Can Sink a Startup*[1] suggests:

- Bringing in co-founders who have the technical expertise, sales background, or social connections that you lack.
- Creating a more diverse team gives you access to a wider, more diverse network (i.e., similar people tend to have similar networks).
- Avoiding co-founding with friends and family; the eventual conflict far outweighs the value.
- Creating a clear division of labor helps accountability and creativity to flourish.
- Having a plan to address problems. Don't avoid conflict; plan for it.

As with serial entrepreneurs, a team with prior work history generates confidence for investors. YouTube founders Chad Hurley and Steve Chen sold their video startup to Google for more than

$1.5 billion. It is no surprise that investors (and the media) paid attention on September 12, 2011, when the duo decided to take over the flailing social bookmark venture Delicious. Similarly, when the franchise czars behind Boston Pizza, Jim Treliving and George Melville, took over Mr. Lube, the world noticed. While experience doesn't guarantee success (Delicious has changed hands several more times), it gets investors' attention.

Investors like reducing the riskiness of their investments by working with entrepreneurs who they have been in battle with before. Investors can eliminate some of the uncertainty around how a founding team will communicate and respond to adversity if the investor has previously worked with the team.

Founder's Perspective: Circa
By Matt Galligan (Co-Founder)

At the end of 2011 when Ben Huh and I came up with what Circa would become, it was extremely clear to us that reading news hadn't had any sort of leap forward ever, really. Sure, there are more articles, they arrive faster, and we discover them differently, but at a fundamental level, the actual consumption experience was no different. At the core of the problem was this concept we called "news amnesia"—every day new articles came out that referenced yesterday's news and often repeated a lot. This is called "background." But what if I didn't need that background? What if I still knew what happened yesterday? Every article serves two audiences: those who are new to the story and those who have been keeping up. Circa ended up pioneering something we called "follow" to solve this problem and get continual updates on stories that move forward. We took our knowledge of the concepts behind software engineering, version control, and object-oriented programming and applied those principles to software for writing and reading news. Blending tech, product, and news content is still something out of reach for most news outlets.

While working through the concepts that would become Circa, we kept getting asked, and asked ourselves, a fundamental question: "Why hasn't this existed yet?" The idea was simple enough: Make it easy for people to stay on top of the news stories they care about by allowing them to follow them like people follow other users on Twitter. The more we dug into the problems, the more we realized why no one in news had done it yet: because our solutions went against the way news was traditionally made, something that most of the industry and the people within it are completely indoctrinated in. We established early on that there was nothing sacred and that we should break down the ideas to their core and then build them back up in a way that we as consumers wanted. Our follow feature is still unique two years after launching

(Continued)

(*Continued*)

because while the concept may be obvious, the barriers to recreating it are high, both technologically and culturally.

Everyone needs to be informed about the happenings in their world. News wasn't going away. But news was also not evolving. The structures for reading and writing were largely the same as they were a century ago. When evaluating what opportunities could be chased, how exciting would it be if we could make even a minor dent in such a legacy business?

Investor's Perspective: Circa
By David Cohen (Techstars)

A great investment opportunity stands out when it's the combination of the right idea and the right people to execute on that idea. Opportunities will often emerge out of long-term relationships that you've developed over time. When you gradually get to know someone, watching them learn and evolve and confront challenges, you get a sense of what kind of person they are. When you trust in someone's abilities, creativity, and character, you can trust them with your investment.

Most seed investors invest in people. In Circa's case, that person was Matt Galligan. He was in the first Techstars class in 2007, and since then, I've gotten to know him very well. Circa was Matt's third company, and the third one that I invested in. After he very successfully sold his first company Socialthing to AOL, I invested in his second company, SimpleGeo. While SimpleGeo was not a success, Matt was a good steward of our investment and sold the company to Urban Airship, which has grown nicely and will produce a great return.

In 2011 at Techstars FounderCon, our annual founders conference of Techstars mentors and alumni, Ben Huh, CEO of the Cheezburger Network and a Techstars mentor, had an idea for a media company and announced he was looking for someone to run with his idea since he was busy building Cheezburger. Matt jumped at the opportunity. It was such an awesome way to get a great idea off the ground and turn it into a reality. That's what can happen when you're able to leverage the power of a strong network to collaborate and bring ideas to fruition. Ben was a co-founder and was active as a member of the board of directors of the company.

Circa is a clear combination of the right idea and the right people. Matt is very good at product vision and evangelism, and he put together an outstanding founding team of people with excellent track records. Along with the team, the idea and opportunity behind Circa attracted me. By capitalizing on the trend of mobile first, the product combines the way people use their mobile devices with news, content that everyone wants. The novelty of Circa is that it thinks about the news consumption pattern differently, allowing people to read news that matters to them quickly and at a time that is convenient.

It's a terrific idea and that was important in my decision to invest, but the most influential factor was the relationship I already had with Matt and my trust in the people who would oversee making the idea happen.

Working Full Time

Full-time commitment to the new opportunity matters. If the number of full-time founders is zero, you have a problem. Remember, ideas don't count. Execution counts and execution requires focused founders. If no one is working on this opportunity full time, how will it make progress? The more people who are all in and working exclusively on the opportunity, the greater the chance that you have for success.

Working on a new opportunity full time demonstrates commitment. If you can't do that, consider other ways you can show commitment. Investors want to see what is commonly called "skin in the game"—the idea that founders have something at stake in the outcome of the company.

Some investors are hesitant to invest in something that the founders won't commit to full time. But many founders need funding to afford to be able to focus on the opportunity, resulting in a big Catch-22. So, what do you do if you aren't ready to quit your day job? If you can show that your product already generates revenue or users while you are working on it part time, then you can make a credible case that taking on investment and going full time will propel you to greater success. While it's always important to show early proof of your concept, this is even more important when you can't commit full time to your opportunity.

Been There, Done That

All great entrepreneurs learn from their previous mistakes as well as their successes. Experience comes in many forms, including leading a startup through a successful exit as well as getting a startup off the ground only to have it crash and burn.

Different founders have different experiences. By building a team that has a diverse set of backgrounds and experiences, you can accelerate the opportunity evaluation process since each founder brings different lessons to the party.

This is especially important in situations where you are a first-time founder. Rather than try to figure out everything by yourself, find a co-founder who has some experience. If you are a first-time founding team, find mentors who can work with you from the very beginning of the business. If you don't have experience, attract it to the team and include it in what you are doing.

Investors often say, "I don't want founders learning on my dime." While many investors feel that backing an experienced entrepreneur is a safer investment, others love to work with first-time entrepreneurs. While experienced entrepreneurs are often viewed as having more realistic projections and timelines, better access to resources, including capital, and more seasoned judgment, first-time entrepreneurs will often be more creative and not constrained by prior experience. The combination of first-time and experienced entrepreneurs on the same team can be magical.

Passion

Starting a business is extremely hard. Resources are scarce. Obstacles abound. Success is elusive. The only guarantee in a startup is that you will work hard all the time for many years.

Entrepreneurship is a calling, not a job. You should only work on opportunities you are extremely passionate about. A famous golfer once said that people only do their best at things they enjoy. This is true as much for entrepreneurship as it is for sports. Passion for profits is not enough to keep you going in the middle of the night.

Solving problems that you yourself have—scratching your own itch—is a powerful approach. Couple, a successful app that allows two people in a relationship to privately and securely share intimate communications, was born of personal need. While Michael Petrov and his fellow co-founder were at Y Combinator building the initial prototype for Couple (originally called Pair), their girlfriends were back in Canada and Japan. The strains of a long-distance relationship led the Canadian founders to focus on creating a platform for connection with their girlfriends. This idea resonated so much that within the first four days of the beta launch of the app, they had over 50,000 downloads and had facilitated more than one million messages. When interviewed on Sean's *The Naked Entrepreneur*,[2] Petrov was asked how young student founders can find their passion. His response was laser-focused; he told the student audience to focus on their fervor. Explore and build what you would do on Thursday night if you weren't going out to be social at the university pub.

Founders will invest many thousands of hours into building their company. Before doing so, ensure you are going to love—not like—the idea. If you choose your opportunity based on potential monetary gain, what will you do when that money doesn't arrive? Don't focus on the financial outcome. Instead, choose your opportunity based on what you are obsessed about.

The notion of "even if I wasn't funded, I'd do this anyway" is a good sign for investors. Matt Canepa and Pat Pezet from Grinds Coffee[3] had this type of passion. The pair raised money for their product, which is a coffee pouch filled with freshly ground coffee. They flavor the coffee pouches and supplement them with vitamins and nutrients. They came up with the idea one night while studying for a college exam and realized it could be a viable and healthy alternative to chewing tobacco.

Passion also has a dark side. Too little passion will undermine your adversity quotient (i.e., your resilience to negative events) and you'll quit before you make progress on an opportunity. Too much passion can make you willfully blind to issues. Successful founders find the middle ground, resolutely believing their vision while staying grounded in the real world. The key is finding the balance between blind faith and rational optimism.

Jim Collins, author of *Good to Great: Why Some Companies Make the Leap . . . and Others Don't* dubbed this balance the "Stockdale Paradox."[4] Admiral James Stockdale was a high-ranking military officer held captive for seven years during the Vietnam War. While in captivity, Stockdale was regularly tortured by his captors. Many of his fellow captives died, but Stockdale told himself he would one day be free and that he would someday get to see his wife again. Stockdale balanced his blind and unwavering faith in future freedom with a grounded understanding of his current reality. It is this precarious balance between faith and optimism for the future on the one hand, and acknowledging the current reality on the other, that characterizes the Stockdale Paradox, and it applies just as much to founders as it does to prisoners of war. To paraphrase Jim Collins in *Good to Great*: Entrepreneurs must retain faith that their venture will succeed, regardless of the difficulties. At the same time, founders must be willing to confront the most brutal facts of their current reality, whatever they might be, balancing commitment with critical thinking, blind faith with objective milestones, and passion with pragmatism.[5]

Coachability

Entrepreneurs require thick skin and resilient egos. Without both, founders would not be able to endure the ups and downs of startup life. All startups need both exuberant passion and stoic dedication. Without perseverance and confidence, most startups won't survive their first year. Often, all a founder has at four in the morning is her passion for the business she is creating. And yet, sometimes too much passion can be a barrier to honest opportunity evaluation.

Pristine Cart[6] is a product that sanitizes shopping carts. The grocery store pays for the product, but the benefit goes to the grocery store's customer. While the idea was clever, the opportunity was flawed because the cost to the grocery store was high and far outweighed the benefit generated, which was mostly goodwill from the grocery store's customers. While there could have been other approaches to Pristine Cart, the entrepreneur was stubborn and refused to acknowledge the imbalance of value, even after hearing it from several potential customers. Part of this stubbornness resulted from the entrepreneur having already invested $120,000 in the product. But when investors also tried to reinforce the feedback that was coming from prospective customers, the entrepreneur's continued stubbornness got him branded as not coachable.

Coachability refers to the founder's openness to review, questioning, and advice. It is not about having the right answer, but about being able to put your own ego to the side and be open to external feedback. A great founder has enough confidence in his idea to actively seek criticism. This is a key part of the opportunity evaluation process since being open to feedback allows an entrepreneur to identify and address potential issues with his idea.

Startups change and few business ideas end up where they started. A founder who is coachable will demonstrate this ability almost immediately. To test coachability, a prospective investor may ask a direct question such as "I'm concerned about Google, why don't you think they are a threat?" and see how the founder reacts. If the entrepreneur responds with "Google has no idea how to innovate . . . ," it may be a sign that his ego is impacting his judgment and that he's not particularly coachable.

When exploring coachability, look for thoughtful, humble, and inquisitive responses. For example, when asked "Where do you see yourself in the company in three years?" you don't want to hear something like "Leading the company. I'm the only CEO we will ever need." Something like "Wherever the company needs me" would inspire much more confidence. Or, in response to the question "Who on your team knows more than you?" a terrible answer is "No one." In contrast, a great answer is "Everyone. I always surround myself with people who have skills I lack." When asked "I'm concerned about Facebook. Why don't you think they are a threat?" an appropriate answer might be "Of course, they could do it. They could do anything. But the relevant question is 'Will it rise to the top of their product development road map in a time frame where they could impact our go-to-market strategy?'"

Firms with almost infinite financial resources can do many things, but they also have structural barriers to rapid iteration around new ideas such as politics, bureaucracy, and prioritization. Our laser focus and intensity around a specific, high-value idea is what will create barriers to entry in the wake of good execution.[7]

Many investors aspire to contribute more than just money to a new company. They want to add their mentorship, their network, and most of all, the lessons learned from their own experience. Investors want to back entrepreneurs who listen as much as talk.

Founder's Perspective: The 7 Virtues Perfume
By Barb Stegemann (Founder)

My passion stems from my gratitude that as a woman I live in Canada, a country where I can freely vote, I can earn money, I am safe, our children can go to public school, our roads are paved, and the list goes on. Raised from humble roots, on welfare for much of my teenaged years, I realized I could get a part-time job, and I could get clothes like the other kids so I could fit in. I also feel we must share what we have with others in a dignified way. I never wanted charity; I wanted to be invited to the banquet. So that is what I have created with the 7 Virtues. We invite our suppliers from Haiti, Rwanda, Afghanistan, and the Middle East to come to the banquet through our purchases of their essential oils for our fragrances. We are equals. I need them and they need me.

(Continued)

(*Continued*)

I am passionate about the 7 Virtues because it has provided me and everyone who loves our fragrance collection with a way to also empower families in rebuilding nations. I deeply appreciate my investor, W. Brett Wilson, who has become my mentor and gives me all the support and room I need to expand and grow our company. We have demonstrated that social enterprise can be excellent, and yet our products are extraordinary by themselves. And that's key for us—that our customers want our fragrances because they do not contain phthalates or parabens and they are vegan. Women tell me they could not wear fragrance before our collection with natural essential oils and they now are wearing it at work!

My passion makes the 7 Virtues a success simply because I respect this idea as much as I respect and value my children. I nurture, protect, honor, push, challenge, and do all the things parents do for their child for the 7 Virtues. No more, no less. I know when to let go and when to apply careful attention.

Investor's Perspective: The 7 Virtues Perfume
By W. Brett Wilson (Investor)

In all my time on *Dragons' Den*, I have never been as impressed as I was with Barb Stegemann. Barb came out, looked us right in the eye, and said, "This is what I'm about." I will never forget that moment. Investing in social entrepreneurship can be hard. Not-for-profits aren't typically good investments. But that wasn't what Barb was offering us. Instead, she was proposing an investment in a for-profit company that would be good both socially and financially. Barb wasn't looking to create charity. She was looking to fuel self-reliability through entrepreneurship.

Barb had passion and resilience written all over her face, which are two things every entrepreneur must have to turn an opportunity into a success. Every day, founders face profound uncertainty and scarce resources. When you are worrying about your company while everyone else is sleeping, passion is the only thing that will keep you going. Similarly, after you experience months of rejection while trying to break into any industry, resiliency is sometimes all that you can rely on. Barb demonstrated unequivocally both passion and resilience during her pitch.

Unlike so many others who come onto *Dragons' Den* looking to get funding for their dream, Barb came in to share an opportunity she was passionate about and dedicated to. She didn't apologize for paying higher than market price for her overseas ingredients because she purchased ingredients from impoverished farmers and then used that high price to allow consumers to feel good about their consumption. Barb turned her constraints into an opportunity. Based on her deep passion for providing the world's poor with a self-empowering solution, I felt compelled to participate. Since that first day when I met this firecracker of a founder, Barb has done nothing to make me regret my decision to support and fund her. Today, more than ever, I believe in Barb Stegemann and her 7 Virtues perfume products.

Ability to Attract Talent

Being able to attract talent is a powerful talent in and of itself. This is especially important when it comes to the founding team.

Most startups are severely resource-constrained and rarely have an abundance of capital or people. Part of the search for capital is to reduce these constraints. But to attract capital, you should have a great team. This may seem like an intractable problem, but great entrepreneurs find ways to build a strong team prior to having capital.

Why would someone forgo another opportunity they already are working on to join your brand-new, unfunded idea? Interestingly, this can be a powerful way to practice explaining your idea, and it can also act as third-party validation of your ability to articulate your vision and the opportunity you see in front of you.

If you can attract other founders to join you instead of staying at their high-paying jobs, investors will want to find out why. If you can recruit people away from their current roles at other companies to join you, it supports the notion that your opportunity, and your ability to explain it, is compelling. Recognize that the negative inference is also valid: If the opportunity is so good, how come no one has quit his job to work on it full time?

When someone is evaluating an opportunity, finding the right talent to add to the mix is crucial. Several years ago, Sean conducted a study for Toronto's *Globe and Mail* newspaper that showed it takes a well-balanced management team to run a successful startup. He came up with a construct that he calls the Talent Triangle,[8] which is made up of three elements: business acumen, domain knowledge, and operational experience (see Figure 5.1).

Let's discuss each element of the Talent Triangle in more depth.

Business Acumen

Business acumen, which is typically found in the CEO, COO, and CFO of a company, refers to the ability to run the business. Do the leaders on the management team know how to budget, forecast, lead, and plan? Can they handle basic business and management issues surrounding a startup?

A founder with business acumen will have spent several years in a senior role at another startup. He will have a sense as to how much

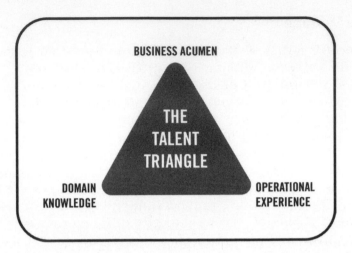

Figure 5.1   Wise's Talent Triangle

money to raise at what time, how and when to hire employees, how to think about intellectual property, and how and when to scale the business.

Without business acumen on the founding team, an opportunity often founders. Business acumen is the result of years of business experience and is typically stage-centric, rather than domain-centric. Specifically, a Fortune 1000 company CEO will not necessarily have business acumen for a startup, while a young founder who is on her second startup will.

Thoughtful entrepreneurs recognize their weaknesses and realize that they are not just asking for money, but are also asking for business expertise. An example is David Koetsch, inventor of Grow Zorb.[9] Koetsch, a design engineer, began seeking funding only after understanding his product, his customers, and his competition. It was clear to investors that David had domain knowledge and operational experience, but lacked business acumen. As part of his pitch, David mentioned he was looking for a partner with business knowledge. When investors finally agreed to invest, one of their conditions for the deal was "We need a person who can run the business in hand, so we've got to recruit that person as quickly as possible." If your team is light on business acumen, recruit lawyers, accountants, and mentors to help early on in this area.

Domain Knowledge

The second corner of the Talent Triangle is domain knowledge, which is obtained by working in the industry in which you are building your opportunity. Domain knowledge starts with knowing your customer and your industry. Do you understand what the customer wants? Do you know how your customer buys? Do you understand which features and benefits are most important to your customer? Do you understand the industry you are operating in, and know about—or at least have hypotheses about—the specific opportunities to disrupt the way the industry traditionally works?

If you want to run a startup that revolutionizes banking, domain knowledge would come in the form of years of experience working in the financial sector, preferably in banking. If you are trying to implement something new, having inside knowledge of how things work in that industry is an important starting point.

In the banking example, a person who previously was the COO of Bank of America wouldn't necessarily have the requisite business acumen, because she has large company, rather than startup, experience. But she would have strong domain knowledge at a software firm trying to revolutionize the back-end processing of electronic banking transfers.

Domain knowledge can also help identify and attract key people as well as help ensure that the startup's go-to-market plan is reasonable and realistic. For example, an executive who has spent two decades in the wireless payment industry will likely know what clients want and what some of the industry's fatal flaws are.

Without domain knowledge, startups run the risk of building a solution that no one wants, often referred to as a solution in search of a problem. Worse yet, without domain knowledge, many startups oversimplify their problem analysis and dramatically underestimate the challenge of building something compelling.

Operational Experience

The third corner of the Talent Triangle is operational experience. Entrepreneurs with operational experience know how to make and deliver a product to a customer. In an online grocery store, this entrepreneur would supervise not only the creation of the e-commerce front-end website, but also the process for the delivery of the food. Operational experience is all about getting the product from design to delivery.

Without operational experience, founders often have trouble launching their product. Or worse yet, they may launch but fail to deliver on their promises. A great product is only great if it reaches end users and customers. If your team lacks operational experience, look for people to add to your team who have built similar products in the past.

Albert and Richard Amini are doctors who went on *Shark Tank* looking for help to build a product called Rolodoc[10] for the medical industry. Rolodoc is a directory of physicians and medical professionals for patients that allows for communication and rapid exchange of ideas. Being medical practitioners themselves gives the founders the domain knowledge they feel they need to take Rolodoc to market. While the Sharks agree that being part of the target market is helpful, the Rolodoc team loses investors when it comes to operational experience. Neither of the founders know the first thing about building, launching, growing, and sustaining a social network business.

Mentors

Mentors, typically experienced entrepreneurs or domain experts, can help entrepreneurs in a wide variety of ways, including identifying issues before they arise, crafting solutions to obstacles based on prior experience, providing a role model for the founder to emulate, and acting as a decision-making sounding board.

Limited resources often prevent entrepreneurs from hiring employees or outsourcing the many tasks they must accomplish, such as marketing, product development, accounting, and human resources management. Novice entrepreneurs must also rapidly develop management skills, a lack of which is often identified as one of the main reasons for a business's failure. Mentors can play a key role in these areas as informal learning and coaching plays an especially important role in the growth of the skills of an entrepreneur.

Being a founder or a CEO of startup can be extremely lonely, frustrating, and full of conflict and disappointment. Simply having a friendly, safe person to talk to about difficult issues can be amazingly helpful.

Board of Directors/Advisors

Entrepreneurship has many maxims that seem to present the entrepreneur with no way out. It's frequently said that to raise money you need a great team. But to have a great team, you need capital. This lack of capital dynamic often inhibits a startup from attracting top full-time employees, leaving the startup's Talent Triangle incomplete.

A good board of directors or board of advisors can help with this and other things, including:

- Providing a sounding board for founders
- Giving regular feedback on issues and initiatives
- Expanding the entrepreneur's network, leadership skills, and expertise
- Signaling to the world that the new venture is worth supporting

This last point is worth exploring further. In economics, signaling theory deals with how one party credibly conveys information about itself to another party. By creating a board of well-regarded people, you signal that the company is worth supporting. When Meg Whitman, the chief executive of Hewlett-Packard and the former chief executive of eBay, joined the board of Zaarly, a startup connecting errands with those available to undertake them, it signaled to the market that Zaarly was an interesting company. Most people assume Whitman, who led eBay to become a worldwide e-commerce success story, knows something about Zaarly's business, and by joining the company as a board member, she is implicitly endorsing it. However, don't follow this approach blindly since simply having a famous executive join your board doesn't guarantee anything. Founders must still build the business.

A board of directors is elected by the shareholders. Directors have what is referred to as a fiduciary duty to the company and have a set of formal and legal responsibilities that are discussed in detail in Brad's book *Startup Boards: Getting the Most Out of Your Board of Directors*.[11] The CEO of a startup, regardless of whether he is a founder, reports to the board of directors, although there are plenty of cases where a founder can still control the board. Ultimately, directors can be liable for certain actions of the company, so they must take their duties seriously.

Advisors can play a similar role to directors, but without the liability. They don't have the same fiduciary duty to the company and
rarely have any formal or legal exposure with regard to the actions
of the company. In addition, the founders and the CEO can add or
remove advisors at their discretion as the board of advisors works for
the founders or CEO, rather than the other way around.

Customers

One of the greatest paradigm shifts in entrepreneurship over the
last two decades is the role of the customer in new company creation. During the dot-com boom of the late 1990s, investors were
the proof of concept. Instead of being fuel, funding was considered
validation and many entrepreneurs spent much of their time seeking capital. Now, less than 20 years later, customers, not investors,
are king.

There are many reasons why a founder should focus on customers, most notably that customers provide proof of demand for what
you are creating. When a customer is willing to pay for your solution,
even in prototype form, it demonstrates an unmet market need and
can provide an amazing source of early feedback.

Today, the founder's credo has become "launch early, launch
often." Steve Blank and Eric Ries have popularized this idea with
Steve's mantra "get out of the building" echoing throughout startups all over the world. Steve is quick to say that "no product survives first contact with customers," so instead of concocting what you
think is the most brilliant solution to a problem in secret, dump this
approach and get your product or service out in front of customers
as early and as often as possible.

From this perspective, customers become an important part of
your early team. Accessing early evangelist users, early adopters, or
beta testers has become an art form itself, with many recent founders
leveraging a concept now referred to as *growth hacking*.[12] To recognize the changing role of customers, investors often now ask questions around early adopters, including:

- Can we identify potential users and customers?
- Can we access them cheaply and easily?
- What traits do users of your solution share?

In addition to being users, customers are now co-creators. When you upload a video to YouTube, you are co-creating a product that you are simultaneously using. The idea of user-generated content (UGC) has been so important to business that *Time* magazine named "You" the person of the year in 2006. Companies like Facebook, Instagram, YouTube, Amazon, and Google brilliantly leverage their customers as an asset and a co-creator. UGC has spread broadly to all companies, and you now see major brands such as Mountain Dew, Frito-Lay, Nike, and Best Buy using their users to help them with the product development funnel and creative promotion of their products.

Customers have also become a source of key funding for many innovative products through a new approach called crowdfunding.[15] Pioneered by Kickstarter, many other companies including Indie-gogo, Crowdcube, and Betabrand have arisen to further engage customers via crowdfunding. These companies allow for individual customers to commit small amounts of money to endorse the creation of a solution. The Pebble smartwatch is an iconic example as the founders initially failed to secure venture capital. Instead, in April 2012, they posted their idea for a watch that communicates with your smartphone to Kickstarter with a goal of raising $100,000. Within 30 days they logged $13 million worth of preorders, all without having produced the product. Mark Cuban, billionaire entrepreneur and investor on *Shark Tank*, recently opined on the importance of Kickstarter by stating, "Kickstarter should be a requirement for every startup. It's a way for you to create demand and sell the product without giving up any equity."[13]

Social Capital

While parts of your social network might be captured through your social graph on Facebook and LinkedIn, your true social network is not only limited to those people you connect with on these platforms, but also includes friends, family, and the entreprencur you met at the dog park.

Social capital refers to the goodwill contained within your social network. Entrepreneurs with large amounts of social capital will be able ask for help and support from their social network, augmenting the actual capital they have with social capital. Even if you have plenty of money for your company, it may not have the same level of influence as social capital when trying to convince a reporter to write about your business or a prospective customer to do a pilot of your product. Social capital enables entrepreneurs to leverage their relationships to help move their startup forward and make better use of scarce financial resources.

Today, there is growing literature around the concept of social networks. In the last few decades, this literature has explored the benefits and uses of social networks. For example, Mark Granovetter explored how social networks impact job hunting.[14] Granovetter found many job leads came not from your friends and family (e.g., your strong ties), but from friends of your friends (e.g., your weak ties). This became known as the strength of weak ties theory, which suggests that you and your friends and family have access to similar information, while weak ties have access to knowledge outside of your social network.

Entrepreneurs who act as social network nodes with lots of weak connections bring in new information and many strong connections that can help signal success and result in an ability to obtain key resources such as talent. Investors will be more likely to back these entrepreneurs with a proven track record of being able to leverage social capital through social networks.

Investors like to back founders who are both known and in the know. Having a member of your startup who is widely known leads to better media attention and increases how others view your startup. These well-known people can be advisors, directors, or investors in your startup and will add to your social capital. Investors will view this as a powerful resource for your company.

Notes

1. From "A Book in Five Minutes," *Tech Cocktail*, October 14, 2013, http://tech.co/founders-dilemmas-noam-wasserman-2013–10.
2. *The Naked Entrepreneur* with Professor Sean Wise, February 3, 2013, episode featuring Michael Petrov, http://nakedentrepreneur.blog.ryerson.ca/2012/02/03/episode-video-michael-petrov-acquiring-users/.
3. *Shark Tank*: Season 4, Episode 10.
4. Jim Collins, *Good to Great: Why Some Companies Make the Leap . . . and Others Don't* (New York: Random House, 2001).
5. Marten Mikos gives a great interview on this at: http://www.youtube.com/watch?v=KpgnyBD9J5g.

6. *Dragons' Den*: Season 3, Episode 4.
7. Thanks to Roger Ehrenberg from IA Ventures, who posted this answer to Quora. https://www.quora.com/When-pitching-to-an-investor-how-does-one-answer-the-question-Whats-to-stop-Facebook-from-just-implementing-this-feature.
8. Sean Wise, "The Talent Triangle," *Globe and Mail*, May 17, 2006, http://www.theglobeandmail.com/report-on-business/the-talent-triangle/article1099632/?page=1.
9. *Dragons' Den*: Season 3, Episode 10.
10. *Shark Tank*: Season 5, Episode 1.
11. Brad Feld and Mahendra Ramsinghani, *Startup Boards: Getting the Most Out of Your Board of Directors* (Hoboken, NJ: John Wiley & Sons, 2013).
12. For a good overview on growth hacking, read Ryan Holiday's book, *Growth Hacker Marketing: A Primer on the Future of PR, Marketing, and Advertising* (New York: Portfolio/Penguin, 2014).
13. Max Nisen, "Mark Cuban: 'Kickstarter Should Be a Requirement for Every Startup,'" *Business Insider*, January 4, 2013, www.businessinsider.com/cuban-kickstarter-should-be-a-requirement-for-startups-2013-1.
14. Mark S. Granovetter, "The Strength of Weak Ties," *American Journal of Sociology* 78, no. 6 (1973): 1360–1380. See https://sociology.stanford.edu/sites/default/files/publications/the_strength_of_weak_ties_and_exch_w-gans.pdf for the full article.

CHAPTER 6

Pain

"Is your product a vitamin or an aspirin?" is a long-standing startup question. Josh Linkner, managing partner of Detroit Venture Partners, explains on his blog that vitamins increase health but lack immediacy. Thus, vitamins are optional for most people. In contrast, aspirin solves immediate, painful problems, and subsequently, is much easier to sell. Per Josh:

"Businesses that service burning demand and visceral human needs tend to accelerate faster and require far less marketing push than those that offer stuff customers can easily live without."[1]

In economics, the difference between vitamins and aspirin is illustrated by the price elasticity of demand, which explains the variance in the quantity of a product demanded at a certain price. As a product's price rises, you generally see fewer units of the product purchased. When price greatly influences demand, economists say the demand for such a product has high elasticity. Ice cream, fashionable shoes, and real estate all have high elasticity. In contrast, the demand for some products, such as water, air, and basic food is highly inelastic.

Elasticity relates to both price and demand. The more inelastic the demand for a product, the more a buyer will be willing to pay to acquire it. For example, your need to breathe makes the demand for oxygen incredibly inelastic. You would pay any price to breathe. Now, oxygen is omnipresent even though there is inelastic demand. The extraordinary supply results in the price being effectively free except in situations where there is no oxygen available. In those situations, you will pay any price to get some.

If the demand for a product is elastic, then the demand will be very sensitive to price. Consider ice cream. You are probably willing to pay a range of $1 to $5 for an ice cream cone, depending on the brand and amount that is stuffed in the cone. But it's unlikely there is any reasonable scenario where you would pay $100 for the same ice cream cone.

Aaron Marino's product, Alpha M, is a set of DVDs focused on helping men improve their image.[2] Although Marino identified men seeking a better image as an opportunity, he mistakenly believed his solution was an aspirin and not a vitamin. The Sharks didn't agree and informed him that his DVD set is a "nice to have" not a "need to have." They felt the price tag of $297 was too high for them to believe the product would sell.

The demand for aspirin is less elastic than the demand for vitamins. Aspirin is something you need when you have an issue that requires it. In contrast, vitamins are nice to have but not necessary. Aspirin is a pull product, where the customer demands the product. In contrast, vitamins are a push product, where extensive marketing is required to push the product to the consumer.

Juli Deveau and Ozma Khan created Kookn' Kap, a modern version of the traditional chef hat.[3] Kookn' Kap keeps the smell of food out of a chef's hair and keeps the chef's hair out of your food. Deveau and Khan's product solved a small problem for a small niche market, which might be fine as a second stream of income, but in its current configuration it isn't a fundable business. Kookn' Kap isn't a bad product or a poor solution, it just has a small market with minimal growth potential. A business with such a niche opportunity can be a successful small business, but it won't be a scalable or fundable one.

Contrast this with the idea behind Netflix, which is to allow users to watch unlimited video content for a flat fee without late penalties. To some, Netflix is a vitamin that adds enjoyment to their day while to others, Netflix is an aspirin, solving the pain of late fees and desire for immediate access to content. In either case, it has an enormous market.

Value propositions are highly contextual, changing based on who you are presenting to and when you are presenting. In a down economy, aspirin is often all anyone can focus on. In an up economy, vitamins are often popular as people are looking for new things that they don't yet know they need. But in any situation, aspirin is easier to sell than vitamins.

Compelling Unmet Need

Focusing on a clear pain point, or unmet need, is very powerful. The greater the pain, the more likely your product will resonate with customers. You can approach this as a low-cost solution with a very large market or an expensive solution for a niche market. Either way, your customer should view you as a solution to a major problem she has.

In many cases, this pain comes from your own experience. Isaac Saldana, co-founder of SendGrid, calls this "looking for the pain."[4] Kevin Systrom and Mike Krieger, co-founders of Instagram, talk about fixing real problems, stating, "Every startup should address a real and demonstrated need in the world. If you build a solution to a problem lots of people have, it is so easy to sell your product to the world."[5]

Often, this large unmet need isn't obvious. Drop Stop, a company founded by Marc Newburger and Jeffrey Simon, is a car accessory that plugs the gap between your car seat and the center console.[6] The Drop Stop can fit into any car or truck, and it will stop anything from falling into the hole between the seat and console. The Sharks were skeptical until they learned the founders had already sold more than 250,000 units and grossed more than $1.3 million in sales, showing there was a compelling unmet need for Drop Stop even if it wasn't clear.

To scope the aggregate size of an unmet market need, ask three questions: (1) How many people suffer from the pain you are addressing? (2) What is the intensity of the pain each user feels? (3) Is this pain felt once or repeatedly?

Size

Without a large unmet problem, it is difficult to create a significant company. If the pain you are addressing doesn't impact enough people, or doesn't impact people deeply, it will be difficult to gain market traction. If current solutions are good enough, then the pain may not be enough to justify the need for the startup's solution. The number of potential customers suffering from the pain you are addressing is referred to as the total addressable market (TAM). But TAM is not the only factor in the size of your market.

Continuing with the health analogy, let's compare headaches to leprosy. The market for simple headache relief is enormous because the entire world population is susceptible to this inconvenient ailment. Leprosy, while thousands of times more debilitating, has a much smaller total addressable market as very few people contract leprosy. However, the impact of leprosy is much more significant, and the outcome of it not being treated is much more grave than that of a headache. While medication for headaches has a much bigger TAM, the opportunity to cure leprosy could be a much better opportunity because of the inelasticity of price and demand. Someone with leprosy will pay much more for a unit of medicine than someone with a headache.

If the unmet market need isn't solvable but only temporarily stoppable, the size of the unmet need becomes larger. An aspirin solves today's headache, but you don't buy one aspirin, you buy a bottle because headaches return. This return of pain increases the overall size of the opportunity by allowing you to sell the same thing to the same customer multiple times. Consider a car and gas. A car solves the problem of traveling long distances quickly, but once you buy a car that need is met. Gas solves the problem of fueling the car, but you must fill up your car with gas many, many times.

Founder's Perspective: DailyWorth
By Amanda Steinberg (Founder)

DailyWorth.com is the leading women's guide to money and business, and the idea for it struck me like a lightning bolt back in 2008. At the time, I was making $200,000 a year as a computer programmer but had built such an expensive lifestyle that I couldn't afford to pay my mortgage. I hadn't saved a dime, and I was angry that I'd worked so hard to thrive professionally but was overwhelmed by financial stress. I remember around the same time talking to my friend Leah in Los Angeles, who had just been appointed executive director of a well-funded nonprofit with seven full-time employees. She told me she was still unable to pay rent on her studio because she hadn't negotiated a livable salary. Something had to be done for women because our financial woes just didn't seem to match the success we were seeing in other areas of life.

As an entrepreneur in my 20s, I learned repeatedly that businesses only succeed when they solve real problems in the marketplace. I was having too many conversations with myself and women friends about our struggles with money despite our advanced degrees, tireless work ethic, and grandiose ambitions. For an entrepreneur searching for big social problems to solve through business, the signals were too loud for me to ignore. So, instead of talking or continuing to complain about the problem, I decided to do something about it.

I've started six businesses in the last dozen years. Two of them reached over $500,000 in revenue, but didn't scale, so I shut them down. Three others failed due to lack of user adoption. DailyWorth, the sixth, was attractive because it had everything a business needed to succeed: a real problem to solve; a huge, untapped market; a proven and rapidly scalable business model; and a clear path to revenue.

Investor's Perspective: DailyWorth

By Joanne Wilson (Angel Investor)

I was just starting to make investments. Maybe I had made a handful at the point where I met Amanda. I wasn't sure I was even sold on the concept before we had lunch, but my friend Howard Lindzon had invested and asked me to meet with her.

Our one-hour lunch turned into two hours. This is the story everyone tells when they become hooked.

There is no doubt that her timing made sense as more women are becoming responsible for not only their own finances but their family finances. Women are going to make more than their male counterparts at some point. All the statistics are there. Women need communities and conversation around this topic. It is a topic that has been essentially swept under the carpet and that works for men. It doesn't work as much for women. Women like to discuss, get feedback, understand, and probe. The concept that DailyWorth would create a place where women could educate, discuss, and get involved in their own capital made sense.

Yet, it isn't about the idea. I invest in people. Amanda has built several companies. She is an engineer, so she understands product. She can build it. Her tenacity, her intelligence, her ability to articulate what she was building [were impressive] and most important, she had a fire in her belly. Actually, she had an inferno. I said yes, I'd invest before the meal was over.

I got involved, came to board meetings, and to this day, still talk to Amanda and give feedback and advice. As for me, the concept that I should hold back before making another investment ended up not being my thesis at all. My thesis is all about putting money into entrepreneurs who are hungry and passionate about what they are building. When I see that and have a gut feeling that they will figure it out no matter what happens, that is what gets me excited. Of course, I have to understand and believe in the business. At the end of the day, it is all about the entrepreneur.

Durability and Timeliness

In 2008, after Barack Obama was elected president, "Yes We Can!" T-shirts were in demand. Two years later, with the president's approval rating at an all-time low, these shirts couldn't be given away. Thus, the opportunity for Yes We Can! shirts might have been timely, but it was not durable.

In the movie *Back to the Future*, time-traveling protagonist Marty McFly plays the song "Johnny B. Goode" at a 1955 high school prom. His audience is dancing to every beat of his song, the band members have big smiles on their faces, and he's captivated his audience. Then Marty starts shredding on the guitar, sliding across the stage, jumping from the speakers, and crawling along the floor. As soon as he hits the high note, he realizes his audience is staring at him with a look of horror and shock. And then he says, "I guess you guys aren't ready for that, but your kids are gonna love it." Some ideas just hit the market too soon.

The emergence of Facebook and its spectacular rise between 2004 and today coincided with the general population's readiness for social networking along with pervasive computers as well as broadband and mobile Internet. Thus, social networking became a hot market. A market like this is a great thing to be a part of because it leads to such intense demand that frantic buyers are fighting over products. Even if you're not the top business in a hot market, you're still going to do well. In other words, timing matters.

Rock and roll was a hot new trend in 1955. However, shredding and jumping off speakers wasn't widely adopted and accepted until the mid-1980s after punk and heavy metal made those practices part of the rock experience. When launching a new business, the best scenario is one in which you can be a part of a market that is on the verge of turning hot.

You can spot a hot market through the news, water cooler chat, or walking down the street and paying attention to people's behaviors. The signs of changing trends are everywhere. A useful online tool is Google Trends, which lists the top 100 most searched terms in the past day and is a great way to see what people are interested in right now.

In today's global, competitive, and rapidly innovating environment, a founder must not only be quick to market to capture demand, but she must ensure that demand will be durable enough to allow the startup to profit from it. In 1999, many companies were focused on creating software to solve the Y2K problem, and the market for these companies was incredibly hot. By 2001, these companies were largely nonexistent since the problem wasn't durable.

Founder's Perspective: Twilio
By Jeff Lawson (Founder)

We started Twilio to solve our own problem. I'm an engineer and a serial entrepreneur who had started three companies prior to Twilio. I recognized a common thread in my career: As a software person, I saw that the web had opened an amazing array of opportunities to use software to create efficiencies, make markets, and change how industries worked. Yet, with every company, I needed to incorporate communications into a business process or application. Time after time, I never found an elegant, flexible, and software-based means of enabling real-time communications with our customers, our vendors, or our users. It was never clear how to do this without buying big monolithic telco solutions. We suspected that there were many software people like us in the world, people solving problems in their companies who ran into a wall when it came to real-time communications. We confirmed this suspicion with early customer research.

When we sat back and thought about why we'd had this need so many times throughout our careers, it became obvious. Every company communicates—it is core to the human experience. Whether you're communicating with customers or users, between employees, or with your vendors, communications is what makes business happen. As software people, we're rebuilding so many of the world's industries using the web and mobile software. If you ask a developer to dispatch an email when a certain event occurs in her software's workflow, she'd say "no problem." But if you asked the developer to send a text message or initiate a phone call, she'd stare quizzically at you. Even if the developer could make the phone ring or buzz since telecom is geographically bounded, solving the problem in one country leaves the rest of the world unsolved.

However, we didn't recognize the true opportunity until a couple of years into the company, after seeing the breadth of what customers were building and the alternative that they had been struggling with for years before turning to Twilio. A picture began to emerge that telecommunications—a $2 trillion industry—was at the beginning of a once-in-a-lifetime transition from its legacy hardware into a new world of software. At once, it became clear that APIs represent the new dial tone in a software-defined communications world and that we were at the forefront of that migration. That's when the full breadth of the opportunity hit us.

Whenever I have an idea, I bounce it off likely customers or users who have the problem I'm trying to solve. Usually, I would get a tepid response. If I see a trend, then I move in. But with Twilio, we spoke with developers and presented the idea of a cloud-based platform that made real-time communications

(Continued)

(Continued)

an accessible technology. Each time I'd talk to someone, I'd see the gears start turning in our prospective customer's head as he connected the dots between our solution and problems he'd encountered in his previous experiences. After I had that experience play out repeatedly, I dropped what I was working on to pursue Twilio full time and have never looked back.

Investor's Perspective: Twilio
By Chris Sacca (Lowercase Capital)

The publicly switched telephone network is a disastrous mess of legacy equipment and protocols. During my time at Google, I worked on the founding team of Google Talk and learned firsthand how virtually impossible it was for a team without specialized training to integrate into the maze of antiquated interfaces that comprised the prefiber global telecommunications network. As we sought experienced telephony engineers to work on this stuff, we came up short, because many of them had literally retired after logging decades and decades at the incumbents working on infrastructure that hadn't materially evolved in years.

After leaving Google, I took a trip back to my hometown and was helping my dad, a sole practitioner attorney, move into his new office building. A local business had quoted him a couple thousand dollars to set up his phone system. Being mildly technical, I naively assumed that I could dedicate a few hours, get it all configured myself, and save my old man the two Gs. So, I went into his utility closet and was shocked to find a copper spaghetti of dozens and dozens of wires seemingly entangled at random. His office building only had four rooms! I was useless.

In parallel with all of this, I knew that mobile as our primary interface to the Internet was going to explode. I had previously run a group at Google aimed at disrupting the world of wireless spectrum and could see the geometric growth of wireless activity. I had also made an angel investment in Twitter and was advising the company and had a front row seat to the power of SMS at the consumer application layer. It was in that role that I learned how damn expensive it was to integrate text messaging into the service because Twitter had to pay hefty fees to carriers for transporting these otherwise simple messages. If you read up on Twitter's history, you'll learn that SMS fees almost bankrupted the company. In this light, when I met Jeff, I immediately and deeply understood the problem he was solving with Twilio. He and his team had done all the nasty and hardcore telephony engineering so that any developer with a basic knowledge of HTML (read: poseurs like me) could effortlessly include an array of formerly daunting services into their stack. It was as close to magic as I have seen in the realm of code. One of the best demonstrations of this ever was when Jeff would use a mere 10 minutes onstage to live code a Google Voice clone using Twilio's elements, all while talking about the future of the company. Utterly jaw-dropping stuff.

From an investor's perspective, the opportunity to work with Jeff was dreamy. Here you had an accomplished engineer with truly exceptional coding skills. He had exited a company before and then spent time building stuff at scale at a big company. It was clear from day one that he was going the distance with this venture. This would never be a quick flip. He is light-hearted, humble, and self-deprecating. His positive attitude is infectious, and you cannot escape his passion for solving problems. Jeff is one of those founders who leaves you with the sense that the success of his company would be inevitable if we all just busted our asses. My only regret is not having a bigger fund to invest back then.

Notes

1. Josh Linkner, "Aspirin or Vitamins?" Josh Linkner's blog, March 25, 2012, http://joshlinkner.com/2012/aspirin-or-vitamins/.
2. *Shark Tank*: Season 4, Episode 2.
3. *Shark Tank*: Season 5, Episode 3.
4. David Cohen and Brad Feld, *Do More Faster* (Hoboken, NJ: John Wiley & Sons, 2011), 11.
5. Dan Schwabel, "What Gen Y Entrepreneurs Can Learn from Kevin Systrom," Forbes.com, June 27, 2012, www.forbes.com/sites/danschaw-bel/2012/06/27/what-gen-y-entrepreneurs-can-learn-from-kevin-systrom-interview/.
6. *Shark Tank*: Season 4, Episode 20.

Product

Steve Jobs is famously quoted saying that he didn't listen to customers because they don't know what they want. The actual quote is more nuanced.

> This is what customers pay us for—to sweat all these details so it's easy and pleasant for them to use our computers. We're supposed to be really good at this. That doesn't mean we don't listen to customers, but it's hard for them to tell you what they want when they've never seen anything remotely like it. Take desktop video editing. I never got one request from someone who wanted to edit movies on his computer. Yet now that people see it, they say, "Oh my God, that's great!"[1]

Many businesses operate under the principle that the customer knows best and whenever you are working on a new product or idea, you should start with a lot of customer research, focus groups, and market data. Clearly, this conflicts directly with Jobs' point of view. Thus, many entrepreneurs ignore the conventional wisdom, especially when they are working on new innovations.

Regardless of which approach you take, there are fundamental ways to understand how and why your product will have value, especially if you are trying to enter an existing market and disrupt incumbents.

The 10× Rule

The 10× Rule dictates that your solution should be at least 10 times better than current products to overcome the position of the existing market leader. Being slightly better, faster, stronger, or cost efficient is not enough. Having an idea that someone will agree to pay for is a nice start, but the way you make it so everyone will pay for it is to focus on the 10× Rule.

Consider several 10× solutions. Email is pervasive because it is more than 10× faster than traditional mail, which is so slow in comparison that it is now referred to colloquially as snail mail. Wikipedia has over 10× more articles than the *Encyclopedia Britannica*. Amazon has over 10× the number of books as the World's Largest Brick & Mortar Bookstore[2] (located in downtown Toronto, Sean's hometown). The original Apple iPod held more than 10× the songs of a Sony Walkman. Remember the fast-growing Instagram example from earlier in the book? When asked about adoption and the criticism that Instagram was a feature and not a product, co-founder Kevin Systrom told Chris Dixon during a *TechCrunch* interview: "You have to go after a small, targeted problem that you're going to solve better than anyone else."[3]

Google's approach to a search engine was 10× faster than the incumbent search engines while generating 10× better results. Google Docs started off free, which was an infinitely lower price than the cost of the incumbent solution of Microsoft Word. The Amazon Kindle, when combined with Amazon.com's huge selection, completely disrupted the existing publishing industry by offering immediate access to hundreds of times more books on a device you can now fit in your pocket. Being an order of magnitude better at something is a powerful lever.

This exponential level of disruption is referred to by entrepreneurial scholars as *creative destruction*, and, per Joseph Schumpeter,[4] it lies at the heart of true entrepreneurial innovation. Schumpeter theorizes that new exponentially better solutions are adopted so thoroughly that they destroy the existence of prior market leaders.

A powerful example of how the rapid adoption of new innovations creatively destroys existing market giants is the story of Netflix vs. Blockbuster. Netflix's business model was originally based on DVDs rented online and sent by mail and had no late fees. When Netflix's business evolved to always available, video-on-demand streamed over the Internet, Blockbuster's days were numbered. Why go to a video store? Why pay late fees? Why put up with not finding the movie you want? Why leave your couch to figure out what movie you want to watch? Netflix was rapidly adopted, and within half a decade Blockbuster was bankrupt.

Rate of Adoption

The rate of adoption is a measure of the percentage of the total available market that has adopted the new solution. Disruptive technologies follow Everett Rogers' (1976) Diffusion of Innovations theory,[5] illustrated next.

Rogers' Diffusion of Innovations Theory

Rogers' theory suggests that new innovations are not adopted by a population simultaneously. Instead, adoption of technology follows a definitive path for all innovations, where the time taken to reach market saturation varies. The adoption begins with the innovators and early adopters. This often takes a while as the product is rapidly evolving based on customer feedback. The product begins to have broad applicability when it gets adopted by the early majority and is a market-leading product when the late majority begins to adopt it.

Consider Facebook as an example. The innovators were students at Harvard and a few other schools. The early adopters were students around the United States. The early majority were active computer users, including young adults and technology entrepreneurs. Suddenly, parents started joining. By the time grandparents showed up, we were well into the late majority part of the curve. Market share grew rapidly, but it followed Rogers' curve throughout the process.

Disruptive technologies follow Rogers' curve at different speeds. This pace is correlated with the price elasticity of demand and the 10× Rule since the more disruptive the technology, the quicker the adoption. Consider Figure 7.1, which compares the rate of adoption for different technologies in the United States for the last century. From this, you can see that:

- Speed of adoption of new technology is increasing—6 years for MP3 Players vs. 71 years for telephones.
- Technology is building on itself—we couldn't have the Internet without computers, which we couldn't have without electricity and telephones.
- The bigger the potential impact of the solution, the faster technology spreads.

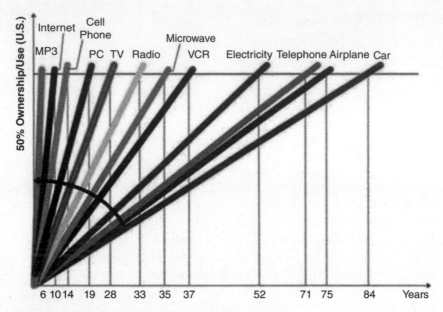

Figure 7.1   Rate of Adoption of Technology in the United States

Source: Data from U.S. Census Bureau, Consumer Electronics Association; Forbes; and National Cable and Telecommunications Association

Intellectual Property

Intellectual property (IP) rights, which refers to a set of legal rights that creators get, plays an important role in opportunity evaluation. An ad man can get a trademark on a cool slogan. The trademark then prevents others from using it. An inventor can get a patent on a novel invention after which anyone who wants to use that invention has to pay the inventor for a period of time. IP law, in theory, is intended to spur innovation by ensuring the inventor gets the fruits of her labor.

IP protection is a subset of commercial law. There are many different forms of IP protection, including patents, copyrights, trademarks, and trade secrets, where the protections vary by the laws of each country. Depending on the type of product you are creating, different IP protection approaches will have different impacts.

A patent protects an innovation that is novel, useful, and nonobvious. Specifically, ideas cannot be patented, only the physical instantiation of an idea can receive a patent. A patent allows the owner exclusive rights to do a specific thing in a particular way for a limited time. After a set number of years, the patent will expire and the solution enters the public domain, meaning that anyone can reproduce it without permission from the patent holder.

A copyright gives the author exclusive right to the work they have created for a period of time. Copyright is most commonly applied to written materials, music, and video creations. Much of the content industry, and infrastructure around it, is built on the notion of copyright.

A trademark gives the owner the exclusive right to use a phrase or symbol. For example, Nike has a trademark on the phrase "Just Do It!" as well as on the iconic Nike swoosh. This is part of Nike's brand identity and can't be used by other companies.

A trade secret is any aspect of a business or product that a company decides to keep secret as a way of gaining a competitive advantage. Trade secrets are often considered confidential information, and a legal document called a nondisclosure agreement is used to protect them when they are disclosed to another party.

Some investors argue that IP protection is necessary to facilitate commercial investment, while others feel that IP laws are outdated and hinder innovation. In today's environment, the historical concept of IP protection, and the impact of it, is undergoing a great debate, especially regarding patents around business processes and software.[6]

Key Asset Access

Some products require access to specific scarce resources. For example, high school gymnasiums can only be rented out to one group at a time. If a necessary asset to provide your product or service is scarce or, worse yet, dependent on access provided by a monopolizing group, you will be at a disadvantage.

The Vancouver-based company Hootsuite is an example of key asset dependency. Hootsuite is a tool to manage a person's Twitter accounts. Not surprisingly, Hootsuite has a dependency on Twitter. If Twitter blocked Hootsuite from accessing its data, or even launched a similar competing service, the opportunity for Hootsuite might disappear. Think that sort of thing doesn't happen? It most certainly does. Many startups try to ride the coattails of larger ventures as a way of leveraging and benefiting from the popularity of the larger company. Sometimes, the larger companies push back.

On September 12, 2014, Kevin Rose launched the app Tiiny to better create and manage small photos and animated jpegs. Tiiny leveraged the large community of users that enjoys and uses Instagram through its "find friends" feature. At least it did until Instagram cut off Tiiny's ability to do so just a few short weeks after launching.[7] This kind of technological protectionism isn't a unique occurrence. Facebook, which now owns Instagram, cut off access to its social graph for startups like Voxer and Vine, which were starting to compete directly with Facebook.

Scarcity drives pricing. If your solution depends on the product of another, then your company is exposed to risk given this product dependency. If the product you are dependent on is scarce, the supplier can dramatically increase the price, resulting in lower margins for your product.

Scarcity can apply to direct resources. A call center typically requires access to minimum-wage employees. A mobile software app developer requires programmers with knowledge and experience with mobile software. A shortage of either of these human resources would exert downward pressure on profit margins.

Proof of Concept—Selling Your Product in Advance of Making It

All entrepreneurs believe in the potential success of their product. To gain an objective perspective, investors often seek evidence that the product is valuable. When Jackie Courtney pitched her business, Nearly Newlywed,[8] she had to convince investors that women would buy secondhand wedding dresses. While Courtney could produce third-party validation of her opportunity in the form of articles from the *Washington Post* and *Inc.* magazine, when she pitched investors on *Shark Tank*, she only had 4 sales in 30 days. While stories in magazines are nice, they are not proof of concept. Investors want to see early customer adoption, usage, and sales.

This is especially powerful if you can get customers to sign up for your product even before it is built. While it's challenging to get someone to buy something before it's ready, the explosion of Kickstarter and entrepreneurs running crowdfunding campaigns in advance of building their products demonstrates that it can be done. A more mundane example is a condominium builder who sells units before a shovel has broken ground. All that is needed are beautiful concept pictures, an empty lot, and a very good salesperson. In turn, the customer can purchase the condo at a discounted price for taking the risk that the condo may not be built exactly as promised.

In addition to confirming the need for your product, preselling your product has other advantages. You can collect cash from the presales, which can fund your product development while reducing the need for financing from investors. You can also engage your early customers during the product development cycle, getting feedback from them early on to improve your product.

Prior to the dot-com bubble bursting a decade ago, proof of concept was analogous to the notion of flipping a light switch and seeing the light go on (i.e., the technology works). Today, more and more investors have expanded the proof of concept definition to be "turn the light switch on, see that the light goes on and that the customer pays something to use it."

During an annual venture fair, where companies come to pitch a panel of investors, Sean once watched a bombastic venture capitalist loudly, and in a very public manner, inform a presenter as to the inevitable fallibility of his company. He stood up and yelled from the judge's table: "This is a stupid idea. No one will buy it. How do you even know anyone cares enough to buy it?" The entrepreneur's answer was calm, confident, and much quieter. The berated founder simply replied, "Because we sold 10,000 units in the first 90 days." Nothing validates proof of concept like actual sales.

Gross Margins

Gross margin is an accounting concept, often presented as a percentage, that represents the difference between the price of the product and the cost of making it. For example, if your product sells for $100 and it costs $40 to make and deliver it, you would have a 60 percent gross margin. The phrase "strong margins" typically refers to gross margins that are both large and sustainable.

The dynamics of margins lie in two additional accounting concepts: average revenue per user (ARPU) and cost of customer acquisition (CoCA or CAC). CoCA is like COGS (cost of goods sold) in that they are both costs that increase as new users are acquired.

ARPU is the amount of revenue from an average user over a period of time (usually annual or monthly). If you are selling a subscription service, the monthly ARPU would be the gross monthly sales divided by the number of customers. If you are selling business legal services, the ARPU would total revenue divided by number of clients served. ARPU represents how much extra revenue you make each time you add a new client.

CoCA is determined from the total sales and marketing costs during a period divided by the number of new customers acquired during the same period. For example, if you spent $100 over a month to acquire 10 customers, your CoCA for that month would be $10.

The relationship between ARPU and CoCA can get very complex and is dependent on the average life of a customer, which ultimately translates into customer lifetime value (CLV).[9] While the absolute numbers of each of these will change over time, if you find that CoCA is greater than ARPU over a specific period, you have an issue.

As an entrepreneur, your goal should be high and sustainable margins, especially over time. While it's easy to talk about revenue, the money you should run your business on is your gross margin. If that number is high, you have greater price flexibility, which, in turn, protects against opportunities that have demand elasticity. In contrast, if you have low margins, you must have massive demand to build a meaningful business.

If a grocery store buys apples at $1 a bag and sells those same apples an hour later for $2, the margin on apples is 50 percent. If that same store buys apples the next day for $2 a bag and sells those same apples an hour later for $3, the margin that day is 33 percent. In each case, the store only made $1, but the risk was higher in the second case since the store would be out $2 if it didn't sell the apples vs. only being out $1 in the first case.

Tan on the Run,[10] a mobile tanning business, had made good profits to date and the founder was hoping to franchise her business. Investors were concerned that it would be difficult to scale her business because the cost to service each customer was high. As *Shark Tank* investor Kevin O'Leary told her, "All the cost of going there, setting up time, then going back, is built into your price. That means you're making 30 percent less than if I set this up on a corner somewhere. You're charging the same and you're doing all this extra work. If you had a fixed location, you could line them up like cattle and spray them down."

A concept called *double dipping* can increase ARPU against a fixed CoCA. When you double dip, you build the product once, acquire a customer, and then sell additional versions of, or add-ons to, the product to the same customer.

A great example of double dipping is Baby Loves Disco.[11] The founders, Heather Murphy-Monteith and Andy Hurwitz, toured the country in a custom disco van throwing incredible parties catering to families. The founders generate revenue from these parties in three distinct ways: (1) ticket sales, (2) merchandise, and (3) sponsorship from family-oriented products. The more parties they throw, the more money each of these revenue streams can generate.

Sean could double dip when he worked on *Dragons' Den* for five seasons. He was paid to support the show, paid again to give keynote speeches about the show, and paid again to transform his experience into content for this book.

Scalability

Scalability refers to an opportunity's potential to bring in revenue faster than the growth of related costs. With a scalable product, margins grow as volumes grow. Software as a Service products are often extremely scalable, as they can add new customers without materially increasing unit costs. In contrast, a law firm is not very scalable because for a lawyer to make more money from his revenue model, he must either: (1) work more hours or (2) charge more per hour.

Scalability has a lot to do with variable costs, which are the costs related to each unit sold, in comparison to fixed costs that are incurred regardless of the number of units sold. The amount of steel used by Toyota Motors is a variable cost. The more cars Toyota makes, the more steel is needed. A highly scalable business will have relatively low fixed costs so that many costs are variable and scale with growth.

Notes

1. Steve Jobs, "Apple's One-Dollar-a-Year Man," *Fortune*, January 24, 2000, http://archive.fortune.com/magazines/fortune/fortune_archive/2000/01/24/272277/index.htm.
2. Not surprisingly, there are several contenders depending on what you consider the definition of "largest" to be: http://retailindustry.about.com/od/famousretailers/f/What-Is-Worlds-Largest-Retail-bookstore-barnes-noblenew-york-powells-portland-oregon.htm.
3. Erick Schonfeld, "Founder Stories," *TechCrunch*, February 3, 2011, http://techcrunch.com/2011/02/03/founder-stories-instagram-products/.

4. Joseph A. Schumpeter, *Capitalism, Socialism and Democracy* (New York: Harper and Brothers, 1942).
5. E. M. Rogers, "New Product Adoption and Diffusion," *Journal of Consumer Research* 2 (1976): 290–301.
6. Brad believes the construct of a patent is invalid in the cases of software and business processes. See http://feld.com/?s=patent for a large number of blog posts by him about this topic.
7. Josh Constine, "Instagram Cuts Off Kevin Rose's Photo App Tiiny From Its Social Graph," *TechCrunch*, October 4, 2014, http://techcrunch.com/2014/10/04/instagram-tiiny/.
8. *Shark Tank*: Season 4, Episode 10.
9. Much ink has been spilled over this concept. One of the best posts is "SaaS Metrics 2.0–Detailed Definitions" by David Skok at www.forentrepreneurs.com/saas-metrics-2-definitions/.
10. *Dragons' Den*: Season 9, Episode 8.
11. *Shark Tank*: Season 4, Episode 19.

CHAPTER 8

Market

Nobel Prize recipient Herbert Simon coined the phrase *bounded rationality*[1] to describe a view of human problem-solving ability. Since we have only so much brainpower and a finite amount of time to apply this brainpower, we can't be expected to solve all difficult problems optimally. Finding the optimal solution often takes more time and resources than would be, well, optimal.

It is more rational for people to adopt rules of thumb to get more out of our limited cognitive resources. The leads to the idea of bounded rationality, where in decision making, rationality of individuals is limited by the information they have, the cognitive limitations of their minds, and the finite amount of time they have to make a decision.

In the world of startups, a bounded market occurs when founders can identify the entire population of users easily. For example, the initial potential Amazon customer population, back when Amazon was starting out with the goal of being "Earth's Biggest Bookstore," was bounded by literacy and access to the Internet. This was a large market, but it became unbounded, or one where the user populations are large, when Amazon expanded beyond books. Consider Google search, which is an unbounded market, in contrast to a search engine that only includes securities-related documents such as EDGAR, which is bounded. Instagram is unbounded, while "the Instagram for doctors"[2] is bounded.

Market Stage

You've just created the best product in the world and it addresses an unbounded market. It's easy for your friends and family to learn about your concept, but how does the rest of the world find out? Unless you're in the movie *Field of Dreams*, "if you build it" doesn't mean that people will start lining up outside your house to buy it. You will need a strategy and an approach to convince customers to purchase your product.

Recall from the last chapter that Rogers' Diffusion of Innovations theory specifies different groups of people that adopt new products at different points in time. Rogers classifies product adoption along a curve representing five distinct stages: (1) innovators, (2) early adopters, (3) early majority, (4) late majority, and (5) laggards (see Figure 8.1).

Innovators, the first 2.5 percent of adopters, often require much more convincing than laggards, who buy because everyone else already has. During most of the twentieth century, it could take a

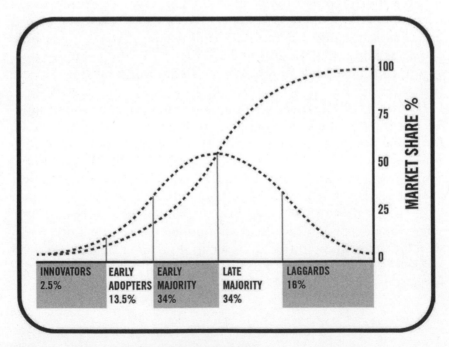

Figure 8.1   Rogers' (1976) Diffusion of Innovations Theory

product decades to move through the entire cycle. More recently, the time frame for these cycles has compressed, and it has become clearer which phase a product is in. For example, consider when you got a Facebook account relative to your friends, parents, or grandparents. The timing of this likely corresponded with the phase of the market Facebook was in.

While early adopters tend to be open-minded and willing to take risks on a new product, getting the early majority on board is often much harder. Yet, the early majority is key to having a successful product since they represent a large percentage of potential users, and once they are on board, the late majority quickly follows. The early buyers of Tesla and Prius cars were almost entirely innovators. As time passed, the early adopters came out in force, at which point other car manufacturers began aggressively promoting electric cars and hybrids. While the "save the planet" message resonated with innovators and early adopters, as we move to the early majority, the message has evolved to include total cost of ownership, especially against the backdrop of high fuel prices, along with better and more contemporary electronics in the car.

In Geoffrey Moore's iconic 1991 book on innovation, *Crossing the Chasm*, he begins with Rogers' Diffusion of Innovations theory and suggests that a chasm exists between the adoption of innovation by innovators and the early majority (see Figure 8.2).[3] Moore believes that innovators and early adopters are technology enthusiasts, while the early majority are pragmatists. Subsequently, these groups have

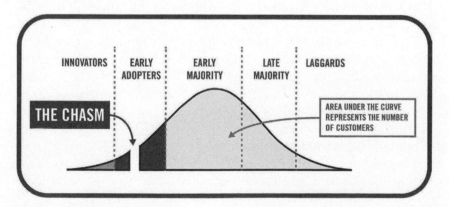

Figure 8.2   Technology Adoption Lifecycle

very different expectations when it comes to adopting innovation, which, in turn, results in a chasm that must be crossed.

Moore goes on to discuss strategies to gain adoption by the early majority. These include:

Piggybacking: When you buy a new computer, there is often a 60-day trial of an antivirus program already installed. Without piggybacking on the manufacturer's existing distribution, the antivirus program would have to rely on you to take the initiative to buy its product.

Industry Placement: Viagra was originally intended to be a heart medication, then later was branded as a sex-enhancing medication, leading to a dramatic increase in sales.

Publicity: When Virgin Mobile launched in Canada, Richard Branson arrived in downtown Toronto in a convoy of Hummers and beautiful models named the "Mobile Revolutionaries" who spread the word of mobile freedom.

When Greg Bay pitched Coretection to investors on *Dragons' Den*,[4] his original target market was injured athletes. The Dragons thought Greg's target market was too small to create a sizable business. Fortunately for Bay, he partnered with Under Armour, an established sporting apparel business. With the Under Armour partnership, the target market for Coretection became all athletes, and Bay's product can now be promoted to help prevent injuries and enhance performance. Coretection successfully piggybacked on Under Armour's already existing brand and distribution channels.

Each stage in Rogers' model requires a different strategy. Entrepreneurs must be mindful to match their strategy and available resources to the appropriate stage. If your product is too far ahead of the market, you will find it difficult to attract enough customers to justify your opportunity's existence and could run out of capital before the market warms to your product. If your product is too far behind the market, you may find your customers buying alternatives instead of what you have created. While having a group of early adopters buying your product is a great start, the real money is made by making your product popular with the majority. To get to the majority, you need to execute a reasonable marketing plan targeted at a specific demographic.

When a new model or approach to a business segment destroys preexisting competition by offering a solution in an entirely new way or to an entirely new market, it is often called a *blue ocean strategy*.[5] The blue ocean strategy of creating uncontested market space is widely seen as the driving force behind many entrepreneurial success stories, including Netflix, Cirque du Soleil, NetJets, Curves, and the Nintendo Wii.

Charles Yim brought a blue ocean strategy to his product the Breathometer.[6] Yim wanted to dramatically expand the market for breathalyzers. Until Yim's startup, breathalyzers were only purchased by police and only succeeded in detecting drivers who were already driving under the influence. Yim felt there was a much larger market than after-the-fact DUI detection as he believed many people would not drive drunk if they knew they were over the legal limit before they got into a car.

The Breathometer plugs into the headphone jack of any smartphone and uses an app to determine the user's breath alcohol content, and correspondingly, his ability, or lack thereof, to drive legally. In doing so, Yim created a new, uncontested market, opening up the segment to anyone with a smartphone. All five Sharks decided to swim in Yim's blue ocean, and he received $1 million in investment, well over the $250,000 he originally sought.

Product/Market Fit

When evaluating an opportunity, you should consider many risks, including market risk and product risk. Up to this point we have largely talked about market and product as distinct concepts. The intersection of the two is referred to as product/market fit and is a milestone that every startup founder strives to reach.

Product/market fit occurs when a startup has found a product that the market will buy. This is rarely a perfect solution, but rather a minimum viable product that customers are willing to pay for.

As product/market fit is the goal, an entrepreneur should have a hypothesis early on of what it will look like. Sean Ellis, a serial entrepreneur, has written on this topic[7] and asserts that if 40 percent of your early users say they would be very disappointed without your product or service, then you have reached product/market fit. A company achieves product/market fit when it has evidence that "sufficient demand in a defined marketplace exists to allow the efficient expenditure of capital to scale company processes such as marketing."[8]

Marc Andreessen, co-founder of Netscape and VC firm Andreessen Horowitz, who is credited with coining the term *product/market fit*,[9] describes this key turning point as the intersection of market pull and firm push. Pushing a product into market refers to outbound sales efforts to drive adoption. Market pull occurs when customers drive the demand for the solution. Andreessen suggests the former is preferable but the latter is within a founder's control. Andreessen believes finding product/market fit to create market pull should be the sole obsession of founders during the early days of any startup:

> Do whatever is required to get to product/market fit, including changing out people, rewriting your product, moving into a different market, telling customers no when you don't want to, telling customers yes when you don't want to, raising that fourth round of highly dilutive venture capital—whatever is required.[10]

Product/market fit occurs only when customers have validated the proposed business model and are willing to buy what you are selling. Per Steve Blank, you cannot move to scaling your business until you reach this point (see Figure 8.3).

A parallel concept that helps explain product/market fit is the idea of evolutionary economics, which uses a methodology to

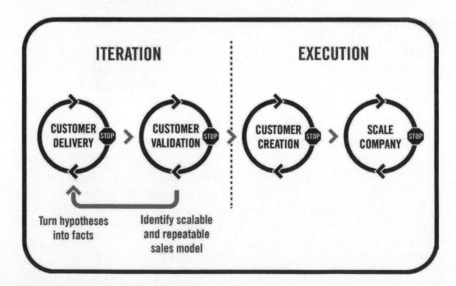

Figure 8.3   Business Model Validation

Source: S. Blank and B. Dorf (2012), *The Startup Owner's Manual.*

understand the processes that transform the economics of firms, institutions, or industries. Like Darwin's theory of evolution, evolutionary economics suggests that only the fittest companies will survive. It is important to note that Darwin did not state that "only the strong survive." It's not the strongest startups that survive but the most adaptable. This is true both in biology and startups.

Figure 8.4 is from a nineteenth-century paper on microbes when S-curve evolution was first discovered. While the S-curve was initially used to explain the behavior and growth of a colony of microbes, it was later shown that the evolution of systems of many different types can be depicted on an S-curve.[11]

An S-curve is produced by the interaction of two processes:

1. The ignition and rapid growth of a chain reaction based on a positive feedback, or reinforcing, loop in a nonlinear system.
2. The gradual weakening of a chain reaction due to exhaustion of the resources necessary for it to "burn," or the emergence of a negative feedback, or stabilizing, loop.

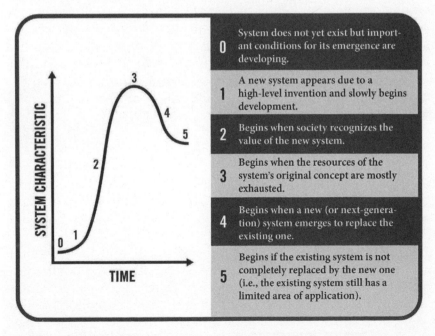

Figure 8.4   System Evolution ("S Curve")

Source: A. Zusman, B. Zlotin, and G. Zainiev (2001), *An Application of Directed Evolution,* Ideation International Inc.

The application of an S-curve works for startups in the same way as it does for hurricanes and microbes. Startups with product/market fit scale up, leveraging massive adoption to generate greater economies of scale until saturation is hit, at which point adoption and the corresponding growth rate begin to slow and taper off.

The power of product/market fit is on display when Kent Frankovich demonstrates Revolights,[12] a product that consists of intelligent rings of LEDs that mount to a bicycle's wheels. Revolights synchronize to the speed of the rider to create a forward-projecting headlight that stays in the right position at any speed, a rear-facing brake light, and a dramatic increase in visibility from the side. Frankovich iterated on his product and used a single online channel to sell more than $600,000 lights in the first year, demonstrating that his product has achieved some level of product/market fit before he went looking for investment.

Disruptive Innovation

Most startups seek *disruptive innovation*,[13] a term coined by Clay Christensen,[14] which describes a process by which a product becomes initially popular in simple applications at the bottom of a market and then relentlessly moves up market, eventually displacing established competitors (see Figure 8.5). Per Christensen: "An innovation that is disruptive allows a whole new population of consumers access to a product or service that was historically only accessible to consumers with a lot of money or a lot of skill."[15]

Industry CAGR

Compound annual growth rate (CAGR) represents the year-over-year historical growth of an industry. The larger the CAGR of a market, the faster that market is growing. Typically, a hot market is one with a CAGR of over 25 percent.

The expression "a rising tide lifts all boats" aptly describes the mechanism here—faster industry-wide growth benefits all those within that industry. Opportunities in industries with a larger CAGR are more attractive to both investors and entrepreneurs. The business of innovation is difficult enough in any market, so why focus on addressing a market that isn't growing? While it is possible to calculate CAGR for an industry, many investors and entrepreneurs simply

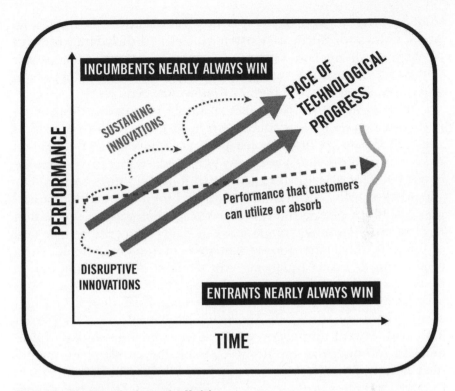

Figure 8.5   The Disruptive Innovation Model

Source: Clay Christensen's Disruptive Innovation Model[16]

go with their gut instinct when it comes to assessing CAGR's impact on an opportunity.

For example, iOS apps, gene theory, and 3D printing are all experiencing huge industry-wide growth right now, with each of these industries having a high CAGR. Compare this to industries such as couriers, record stores, and typewriters, which are all experiencing contraction of their demand, resulting in low or negative CAGR.

Distribution Strength

Distribution strength addresses how easy it is to get your solution into the hands of end users. A great solution can't be adopted rapidly unless it can garner wide distribution, which is one of the great leverage points of the Internet and digital startups since most have solutions that can be globally distributed for low cost. For example, Apple launched iTunes as a system to sell and distribute music in January 2001. Over a decade later, iTunes represents well over half of the entire digital market for music. With such a large share of the market, Apple has incredible distribution strength.

Apple's App Store is another example of creative destruction occurring because of distribution strength. Prior to July 10, 2008, if you wanted your application on a mobile phone handset you needed to successfully complete what many VCs liked to refer to as a "double bank shot." First, you had to sell the mobile operators on why they should allow you onto their handset, and then you had to get end users to adopt your product. Given the glacial pace of innovation of most mobile phone companies, especially concerning their lack of focus on third-party software, this was extremely difficult. Thus, very few applications and games ever made it into the hands of end users. Apple changed all of this with their creation of the Apple App Store in 2008. As of March 2017, there were more than 2.2 million apps available on the Apple App Store, which only had 500 when it launched. More significantly, many other companies followed suit, and you can now find app stores for many digital platforms including Facebook, Google, Microsoft, and Salesforce. Allowing end users to download apps of their choice was only part of the true disruptive distribution innovation. The other part was allowing third-party developers to make such apps easily available, eliminating the need for a double bank shot.

Film is another example of disruptive innovation when it comes to distribution. Assume you were an innovative filmmaker in the twentieth century. Getting your independent film into the hands of potential audiences was extremely difficult. Perhaps you could get your film into a festival. Today, you only need to look at the Netflix catalog or sites like IndieFlix and Fandor to see many smaller independent films skipping the movie theaters for direct-to-audience distribution. These services cut out the middleman (the film distribution house) by going directly to viewers. Peter Broderick, who wrote a fabulous treatise on the impact of this change in 2008,[17] suggests that the new system of film distribution is 10× better because it offers the filmmaker greater control, lower costs, and unmediated access to actual viewers.

The Internet itself is a great disruptor of distribution. In the twentieth century, if you wanted to access the world's encyclopedic knowledge, you had to go to the library and read the *Encyclopedia Britannica*. Now all one needs is an Internet connection and Wikipedia.

Customer Acquisition Costs

Peter Thiel, co-founder of PayPal, discusses the intricacies of distribution in his lecture titled, "If You Build It, Will They Come?" which is available in his 2014 book with Blake Masters, *Zero to One: Notes on Startups, or How to Build the Future*. We borrow from Blake's notes[18] on Thiel's lecture with the following:

- Customer lifetime value or CLV
- Average revenue per user (per month) or ARPU
- Retention rate (monthly, decay function) or r
- Average customer lifetime, which is $1/(1-r)$
- Cost per customer acquisition or CPA

CLV equals the product of ARPU, gross margin, and average customer lifetime. The basic question is: Is CLV greater or less than CPA? In a frictionless world, you build a great business if CLV > 0. In a world with some friction and uncertainty, you build a great business if CLV > CPA.

This math is at the heart of distribution. If it costs you more to land a new customer than that customer is worth, you have a business that will lose more money the more new customers it brings on. As investors, we often see CLV < CPA in the early days of B2B startups. The enterprise-focused startup will spend tens of thousands of dollars in direct and indirect costs to land an early customer, but that early customer will pilot the product for free. Often this is acceptable in the short term because the startup needs the reference customer more than it needs the revenue, but it obviously doesn't work for the long term.

Viral Marketing

Viral marketing is a tool for mitigating CPA. Each time a viral product is used, it is passed on to at least two other users, who each then pass it on to two other users, and so on. This process repeats until, before you know it, thousands of users have experienced your solution.

Andrew Chen, an advisor at startup Quibb, posted this solid tidbit on finding ideal distribution:

> You can figure out the right distribution channel by making sure the product has natural virality. If the channel in which the product spreads is new, you have a strong early advantage and can test the value proposition for new viral users and iterate with experiments until you see rapid acceleration. If you start with some initial traffic from a previous product, service, or piggy-backing relationship, you can accelerate usage quickly.[19]

Hotmail is the classic example of viral marketing. Each time an email was sent through Hotmail, a tag was placed on the end that read "Get your free email at Hotmail." The original phrase is attributed to Harvard Business School professor Jeffrey Rayport and venture capitalist Tim Draper, one of the investors in Hotmail. In short order, this tagline was responsible for Hotmail gaining over 250,000 users each day.[20]

Competition

Every opportunity has competition. Your future customers always have a choice regarding how they choose to solve their problems and address their unmet needs. Competition comes in many forms, which we categorize as direct, indirect, alternative, and status quo. Anything your future customers choose to do, excluding buying your solution, is competition.

Let's take an example that occurs daily in homes across the United States. Suppose your teenage daughter comes home and proclaims, "I need a new pair of Nike soccer shoes." What alternatives do you, the customer, have?

Direct: Companies selling the exact same solution/product/service, which includes a pair of high-end soccer shoes from Reebok.

Indirect: Companies selling to the same customers a slightly different solution, which in this case could be a pair of knockoff soccer shoes on sale for half the price.

Alternative: Solutions other than buying a new product. Instead of buying soccer shoes for your daughter, she could wear her older cousin's soccer shoes. This would meet her needs, but not lead to a sale for Nike.

Status quo: The "do nothing" option. Perhaps your daughter should simply wear the pair of athletic shoes you bought her last year?

Never, ever, believe that your opportunity has no competition. While status quo is often the most forgotten source of competition, it can have the biggest impact because it will always be the case that doing nothing is an option. We've seen hundreds of businesses fail because the do nothing option was good enough for their potential customers.

If your customers have more choices, your product needs to be more compelling. Competition isn't necessarily a bad thing and can help validate the opportunity, educate early adopters, and define and differentiate your opportunity's value proposition. Competition can also provide a baseline against which your startup can be measured, illustrating the need for your product. When your competitors do a poor job of meeting customer needs, they will drive more customers your way. If your competitors outshine your business, they will undermine your sales efforts. Compare the postal service to FedEx and UPS. Who is competing more effectively?

There is no amount of ideal competition. Too little competition undermines investor confidence and interest. Too much competition scares away investors. Hot markets, especially ones being discussed in mainstream media, often attract substantial competition in very short periods of time. Many novel and game-changing opportunities require being ahead of such mass awareness.

Companies that try to reposition themselves into a hot market based on the hype surrounding market leaders are called "me-too plays" and aren't often seen as particularly interesting. One of Sean's colleagues is fond of saying "don't jump on a bandwagon that's standing room only." If your market is already filled with tens of competitors, you should reconsider the market.

Future competition can lead to what Thomas McKnight calls *ambush exposure.*[21] McKnight defines ambush exposure as the possibility that an invisible competitor with extraordinary means and resources could find your product so compelling or threatening that they aggressively dive into your market and help themselves to your customers.

Disruptive innovations can create massively successful companies, such as Amazon, eBay, Facebook, and Google. But in creating a disruptive innovation and in showing the large amounts of wealth it can create, you alert larger companies in your ecosystem to the opportunity and invite an ambush. Amazon's online bookstore was originally resisted by the industry. Borders effectively committed corporate suicide by giving over its online bookstore to Amazon, but Barnes & Noble eventually tried to ambush Amazon through its own online store. Amazon's business was so durable at this point that the ambush failed, like Blockbuster failing to ambush Netflix with a similar online service. In these cases, the disruptive innovations were so powerful, and the incumbents were so slow to act, that the ambush strategy didn't work.

One of our favorite stories of ambush exposure is Google Docs. For years, Microsoft battled with WordPerfect over desktop-based word-processing software. Eventually, Microsoft won and WordPerfect was effectively killed by Word. For a while, Microsoft had an almost perfect monopoly on word-processing software. In 2005, Writely, a cloud-based collaborative word processor that required no license to use, was born. In 2006, Google bought Upstartle, the maker of Writely, eventually renamed it Google Docs, and the market share of Word has never been the same.

The Goliath Paradox

When an entrepreneur tells an investor "we have no competition," the investor usually thinks one of two things.

1. Either this founder doesn't know how to use Google or she lacks business acumen when it comes to analyzing the competitive landscape.
2. The idea must be so wacky and so unrealistic that no else on the planet is pursuing it.

Which is worse? They both are.

When you have a huge market incumbent (e.g., Amazon for online retail or Google for search), is that good or bad for you? The answer is both and that's the Goliath paradox. On one hand, a large successful market leader clearly proves there is a market for solving this problem. On the other hand, a large successful market leader should be displaced and that often requires your solution to be 10× better. In contrast, if no one has offered a solution to the problem you are addressing, consider whether that's because there isn't a market or because there wasn't yet a solution worth adopting. The former will devalue your opportunity; the latter creates the opportunity.

Barriers to Entry

A barrier to entry is a continuous hindrance that deters a competitor from entering your market. If the federal government requires your startup to be licensed, that is a barrier to entry. If your startup has the only supply of a key asset, such as a physical material needed to generate the desired solution, that is a barrier to entry. If you own a proprietary technology, the intellectual property (IP) becomes a barrier to entry. Every company should create as many obstacles as possible to make it difficult for a competitor to enter your market.

According to Harold Demsetz,[22] potential barriers to entry include:

- Market regulations
- Exclusive distribution agreements
- Inelastic demand
- Predatory pricing
- Sunk and switching costs

A common barrier to entry is a patent. A patent gives the inventor exclusive rights to use a specific technology for a specific amount of time, usually 20 years. When Larry Brun pitched the Attitube, a product made up of stabilizing weights filled with water,[23] he took time to explain the unique features of his product. Then he answered the question "Do you have a patent?" Fortunately for Brun, he did have a patent in Canada and the United States, which gave investors the secure feeling that if they invested in the product, the competition could not copy the technology.

Other examples of barriers to entry can include:

Cost leadership: Get your product at a cheaper cost, which allows you to sell the product at a cheaper price. Walmart is historically extraordinary at this.

Customer loyalty: Many people will only use Google as their search engine because they trust that it is the fastest and most accurate. To date, Bing has not been able to break through this barrier.

Control of resources: If you are making bamboo T-shirts and you have a way to control the flow of bamboo, then no competitor will be able to make bamboo shirts.

Barriers to entry add to the cost of market entry, and therefore, serve to enhance an incumbent's market position. For example, the airline industry has large barriers to entry. First, federal regulations are costly to meet. Next, the costs to acquire the equipment needed to launch an airline are extremely high. Finally, airlines must reach agreements with all the airports where they wish to fly. Because of these high barriers to entry, incumbent airlines have a strong entrenched position, and the airline industry is subsequently unattractive to many entrepreneurs and most investors.

When shaping your idea, improve it to a point that is dramatically better than any alternative and protect your idea by establishing barriers to entry. The bigger the barriers to entry, the harder it will be for a competitor to ambush you.

Government Regulations

Does your company require government approval or some type of government-issued license to operate? Many industries are regulated by some level of government and to participate in that market, a license may be needed. Government regulations may require testing, evidence, or even compliance with certain standards. Thus, government regulation can act as a barrier to entry and can significantly impact the cost to launch a product.

In other cases, government regulations may influence how and where you can sell your product. If you wish to open an institutional lending operation like a trust company, most countries require you to meet certain standards (e.g., cash reserves), conduct business a certain way (e.g., can't loan millions to people under 18), and comply with filing requirements (e.g., monthly transfer reports). In some cases, governments restrict you from selling your solution to certain groups (e.g., anti-money-laundering rules).

Partnership Status

Does your startup have potential partners? Do you know any of them by name? Do these partnerships materially increase either your confidence or the probability of success for the startup? If yes, then the venture is experiencing what scholars call the *halo effect*.[24] The halo effect occurs when one entity—either a company, investor, or celebrity—tacitly endorses another by agreeing to work with them. Many startups use the halo effect as a form of proof of concept.

Under signaling theory, the halo effect caused by partners is an endorsement. Consider the following:

Startup XYZ is in the search industry. It claims to have invented a way to search images, something the search industry has struggled to address for a long time. On day one, the founders pitch investors "the solution to image search," but the live demo fails and investors lose confidence in the opportunity. The next day, the founders of startup XYZ announce they have entered a partnership with Google to leverage their IP and expand the market. Regardless of how investors felt before the announcement, Google's signaling and halo will raise the level of interest in the opportunity.

While customers are the best testament to an opportunity's potential, what can you do if sales are not yet forthcoming or your startup is prerevenue? In these cases, the next best proof of concept comes from partnerships with highly credible entities. Partnerships can come in all shapes and sizes, but generally the ideal partnership will see the partner allocating resources to enhance the probability of the startup's success. Partnerships should advance the progress of the company while increasing the confidence an investor has in it. After all, if a big company thinks your company has value enough to partner with you, then maybe there is something there.

As investors with a focus on digital startups, we don't know much about pharmaceutical R&D. But if a startup came to us with several large, relevant partners already on board, including a leading hospital, a well-known lab, a famous university, and a large public pharmaceutical company, we would be more confident about the opportunity.

Knowing Why You Need to Raise Money

To realize the value of the startup, shareholders need an *exit*, a term used to define the moment that the shareholders, including the founders, investors, and employees, can cash out. Most startups typically exit in one of four ways: (1) acquisition, (2) initial public offering (IPO), (3) stock buyback, or (4) bankruptcy.

An acquisition occurs when another company buys the startup by acquiring all the shares or the assets of the startup. An IPO occurs when a startup lists its equity on a public market or stock exchange. A buyback occurs when the startup has enough free cash flow to buy back the shares of investors and founders. The final and least satisfying type of exit is a bankruptcy. It's worth noting that fewer than 2 in 10 venture-backed companies have a successful exit, meaning more than 70 percent of these investments fail to return any money to the investors.[25]

Many entrepreneurs raise money to fund the growth and development of their companies. Some entrepreneurs want the money to launch a marketing campaign, others want to franchise their business, while some need to build more product. While it might be clear to the entrepreneur why he needs funding, investors want to know how their investment is going to translate into more value.

It is up to the entrepreneur to effectively communicate how he can generate a return for the investor. If an investor asks, "Why do you need my money?" a mistaken response would be, "We need your $200,000 to grow our business." A better answer is, "Your $200,000 will enable us to fulfill a recent order of 50,000 units of our product. The gross margin from the order alone will total $500,000." With the first response, the entrepreneur is just begging for money, with no plan on how to spend it. In the second, the entrepreneur has outlined a clear path for the company to make a profit and build more value.

When early-stage investors make an investment, they aim to make a substantial return, often at least 10 times their money within a decade. One way they can make money on an investment is through dividends, which is a share of the profits, but it is unlikely this will total anywhere close to 10 times their investment. More commonly, a large exit results from either the sale of the company or an IPO. Occasionally, investors have an opportunity to sell their shares back to the company, or to a new investor, in situations where the company has grown substantially.

On day one, all startups have the chance at a future exit, but some opportunities are more obvious than others. When a company has IP, market traction, and a sustainable competitive differentiation in a rapidly growing market with large barriers to entry, it is setting itself up for a successful exit. By locking up distribution, creating high sunk costs, and protecting key IP, a company can increase the probability of a successful exit.

Articulating the future value of your company to investors is intrinsic to your startup and should be the goal of all entrepreneurs. Likewise, investors want to invest their money, watch it grow, and then get back a multiple of what they've invested.

Founder's Perspective: Talbott Teas
By Shane Talbott (Founder)

It all started in my hair salon. I wanted to create a special experience for my clients so I shared my personal passion of creating unique blends of tea. My clients loved the tea so much, they kept asking to buy some. I gave away my blends, such as a green tea with strawberry and rhubarb, in small Ziploc bags. My partner, Steve, encouraged me to use my creativity to create packaging and sell the tea blends in our spa.

Talbott Teas started as a business of leisure and shifted into a passion project. Over time, I realized that what we created with Talbott Teas was more than just a product—it was a brand of boutique tea—a small, yet luxurious indulgence. Stores and customers showed so much support for the product that my partner and I sold the salon and focused on building Talbott Teas.

They say that there are no silver bullets in life. However, in a life-changing moment, Oprah put Talbott Teas on her last Favorite Things show, and Talbott Teas moved from being a small business run out of our kitchen and spa to a successful company with more opportunity than we could imagine. However, our opportunity was met with serious funding issues. We couldn't fund the inventory to fulfill orders from major retailers like QVC, Four Seasons, and Bloomingdale's. Trying to grow a business in the recession was miserable. Despite our having huge purchase orders, every bank turned us down for a loan. So, we applied to *Shark Tank* in the hopes of getting an investor to follow the exciting trajectory we were on.

We went on *Shark Tank* hoping to get a deal with Barbara Corcoran, thinking that surely she would appreciate what we were doing. We were surprised and not hopeful when we showed up to the pitch to see Lori Greiner in Barbara's chair. To our surprise, Daymond John, founder and CEO of FUBU, was amazingly supportive, but couldn't invest because he was invested in a competing business. Kevin made us an offer for a higher equity stake than we were comfortable with. We negotiated, and despite him saying that he would not negotiate because he was a disciplined investor, he lowered his original offer and we made a deal.

Next to Mark Cuban, Kevin was the least likely Shark we could imagine who would show interest in a company like Talbott Teas. But, in his Kevin O'Leary "Let's make some money" kind of way, he then teamed with Daymond to broker a deal for us with Jamba Juice.

(Continued)

(Continued)

Having two Sharks join forces after the show and help Talbott Teas get acquired by Jamba Juice was a dream come true. Never in our wildest dreams did we think that we would experience such luck stemming from passion, hard work, and a lot of risk taking. It felt like the best kind of luck—when opportunity meets tons of preparation. From *Oprah* to *Shark Tank* to Jamba Juice, we feel like we are living the American dream come true.

Investor's Perspective: Talbott Teas
By Kevin O'Leary (O'Leary Ventures)

I knew I liked Shane and Steve the minute they stepped into the *Shark Tank*. They were beaming with enthusiasm and passionate about their product—two of any successful salesperson's best assets. That said, I'd never make a deal with somebody just because I like him or her. I've met many business owners who come on *Shark Tank* with infectious personalities and amazing entrepreneurial spirit, but when it comes down to the bottom line, the money isn't there.

Luckily, Shane and Steve backed up their first impression with cash flow. After hearing that these guys grew Talbott Teas from $100,000 to over $500,000 in sales over just three years (with 50 percent profit margins to boot), I knew I wanted in. I always say, "The numbers never lie," and in this case, the numbers were screaming, "Invest, invest, invest."

Then, of course, there was the unique appeal of the market space. Tea is what I call a "recession-proof industry." Caffeine is America's number one drug, and over time, it has proven to be an addiction that endures the fluctuations of the economy. The only thing I love more than a business that's making boatloads of cash is a business that has the potential to continue making boatloads of cash for the foreseeable future.

I saw that potential in Talbott Teas and clearly I wasn't the only one. Just months after we joined forces, Talbott Teas closed a deal with one of the biggest beverage companies in America and was acquired by Jamba Juice. From day one, Shane and Steve were committed to their plan of eventually selling Talbott Teas to a larger company for millions of dollars, an exit strategy that I fully endorsed. They managed to make this happen sooner than anybody expected.

Notes

1. Herbert A. Simon, *Models of Bounded Rationality: Empirically Grounded Economic Reason*, vol. 3 (Cambridge, MA: MIT Press, 1997).
2. Yup, this exists. It's called Figure 1. See Rebecca Borison, "There's Now an Instagram for Doctors," *Business Insider*, June 19, 2014, www.businessinsider.com/figure-1-instagram-for-doctors-2014–6.

3. Geoffrey A. Moore, *Crossing the Chasm: Marketing and Selling High-Tech Products to Mainstream Customers* (New York: HarperBusiness, 1991).
4. *Dragons' Den*: Season 2, Episode 4.
5. Renée Mauborgne and W. Chan Kim, *Blue Ocean Strategy: How to Create Uncontested Market Space and Make the Competition Irrelevant* (Boston: Harvard Business School Publishing, 2015).
6. *Shark Tank*: Season 5, Episode 2.
7. Sean Ellis, "The Startup Pyramid" from Startup Marketing blog, www.startup-marketing.com/the-startup-pyramid/.
8. Tristan Kromer's response to "How Do You Define Product Market Fit?" on Quora, April 7, 2014, www.quora.com/How-do-you-define-Product-Market-Fit/answer/Tristan-Kromer?srid=uh2K&share=1.
9. Marc Andreessen, "The Pmarca Guide to Startups, Part 4: The Only Thing That Matters," June 25, 2007, http://pmarchive.com/guide_to_startups_part4.html.
10. Marc Andreessen, "Product/Market Fit," Stanford University EE204 Class Notes: Business Management for Electrical Engineers and Computer Scientists, June 25, 2007, www.stanford.edu/class/ee204/ProductMarketFit.html.
11. G. S. Altshuller, *Creativity as an Exact Science: The Theory of the Solution of Inventive Problems*, trans. Anthony Williams (Amsterdam: Gordon and Breach Science Publishers, 1984).
12. *Shark Tank*: Season 5, Episode 19.
13. Clayton M. Christensen and Joseph L. Bower, "Disruptive Technologies: Catching the Wave," *Harvard Business Review*, January 1995, https://hbr.org/1995/01/disruptive-technologies-catching-the-wave.
14. Clayton M. Christensen, *The Innovator's Dilemma: When New Technologies Cause Great Firms to Fail* (Boston: Harvard Business Review Press, 1997).
15. Ibid.
16. "Disrupting New Growth through Disruptive Innovation," Innosight, www.innosight.com/services-expertise/expertise/disruptive-innovation.cfm.
17. Peter Broderick, "Welcome to the New World of Distribution," first appeared in indieWIRE, September 16 and 17, 2008, www.peterbroderick.com/writing/writing/welcometothenewworld.html.
18. Blake Masters, "Peter Thiel's CS183: Startup—Class 9 Notes Essay on If You Build It, Will They Come?" Blake Masters's blog, May 4, 2012, http://blakemasters.com/post/22405055017/peter-thiels-cs183-startup-class-9-notes-essay.
19. Andrew Chen, "How to Build a 'Distribution-First' Startup," Quibb.com, http://quibb.com/links/how-to-build-a-distribution-first-startup.
20. "9,000 Uniques in One Day: A Viral Marketing Case Study." Moz Blog, November 6, 2013, http://moz.com/blog/9000-uniques-viral-marketing-case-study.
21. Thomas K. McKnight, *Will It Fly? How to Know if Your New Business Idea Has Wings . . . Before You Take the Leap* (Upper Saddle River, NJ: Prentice Hall, 2003), p. 89.
22. Harold Demsetz, "Barriers to Entry," *American Economic Review*, 72, no. 1 (1982): 47–57.
23. *Dragons' Den*: Season 3, Episode 6.

24. See Richard E. Nisbett and Timothy DeCamp Wilson, "The Halo Effect: Evidence for Unconscious Alteration of Judgments," *Journal of Personality and Social Psychology*, 35, no. 4 (1977): 250 and Lance Leuthesser, Chiranjeev S. Kohli, and Katrin R. Harich, "Brand Equity: The Halo Effect Measure," *European Journal of Marketing*, 29, no. 4 (1995): 57–66. See also Phil Rosenzweig, *The Halo Effect and the Eight Other Business Delusions That Deceive Managers* (New York: Simon and Schuster, 2007).

25. Deborah Gage, "The Venture Capital Secret: 3 Out of 4 Start-Ups Fail," *Wall Street Journal*, September 20, 2012, www.wsj.com/articles/SB100008723963904 43720204578004980476429190.

CHAPTER 9

Plan

Steve Blank is famous for paraphrasing Field Marshal Helmuth Graf von Moltke on his blog and reminding us that no business plan survives first contact with the customer.[1] Many mistake Blank's (and Graf's) instruction and go only partway. These founders ask their customers what they want. That approach is not sufficient. Instead, entrepreneurs should present potential customers with choices and let them show their opinion with their wallets.

There is a secondary message in Blank's warning, which is that business plans are only a starting point. You should execute on those plans, and due to high levels of uncertainty, continuously evolve and adapt the plan on the fly. Darwin was correct—those who can adapt will survive, not just in nature but in the startup jungle as well.

LAUNCH EARLY AND OFTEN
By David Cohen (Founder, Techstars)[2]

A product that nobody uses is like a tree falling in the forest when no one is around to hear it. Maybe it makes a sound, maybe not—but really, who even cares? The same goes for your product. It could be the coolest idea ever, but if no one is around to use it, who cares? If actual customers aren't using your product or service, there's no way to know what's working and what needs to be changed. Keep in mind that the product launch and the marketing launch are two separate things. Your marketing launch can wait. It's fine to delay making a lot of noise and promoting your company in the media until you have good product/market fit and customers love the product. But to get to that point, the product itself should be launched early and often.

(Continued)

(*Continued*)

Are you waiting for it to be perfect, or even respectable? Stop waiting. As Matt Mullenweg says in *Do More Faster*:[3] "If you're not embarrassed when you ship your first version, you waited too long." You need to get your product out there so you can get the feedback that will make it better. If you're working to create something that addresses your customers' needs and solves a problem for them, they'll probably be more than willing to share their opinions. Along with verbal feedback, the ways they use the product might reveal a specific need that you didn't even know existed.

Meanwhile, you're also developing and refining your customer base. Even if your actual product changes dramatically over time, those early customers can become your biggest fans and advocates. Then, when it's time for your big marketing launch, there will be plenty of people around who care about the noise you're making.

Time to Launch

The longer it takes to launch, the more chances there are that something will go wrong. If you are hoping to build an application for the iPhone, then your time to launch ends with the listing of your app in the App Store. The longer it takes to do that, the more chances there are for competitors to undermine your opportunity and beat you to the punch.

Many new companies focus on establishing a beachhead when they get started. A *beachhead* is a military term for establishing a foothold on the ground before launching a full attack. In the world of startups, a beachhead refers to a small, easily accessible, and manageable initial target.

By establishing a beachhead, the startup can generate early feedback before investing deeply in a go-to-market plan. Facebook started with a small beachhead—a single university (Harvard). As Facebook expanded, it limited early users to those who had an .edu email address through their university or college. This allowed the founders to create a minimal viable product geared toward addressing an unmet need in a manageable target market—in this case, students—while establishing a beachhead to expand from.

To instill confidence in your go-to-market plan, consider which target market could be an ideal beachhead for you.

Plan to Scale

As an entrepreneur, you are trying to find a business model that is repeatable, sustainable, and scalable. As we discussed earlier, scaling occurs only after a business finds its product/market fit. This normally is well past the opportunity evaluation phase, but that doesn't mean you can ignore scaling in the early days. If you can't figure out a plan to scale during the opportunity evaluation phase, you should not proceed.

Once you have found your business model and product/market fit, you will begin to scale. This is a process that includes adding incremental revenue without adding incremental costs. If scaling your startup results in increased costs without additional returns, then the company is prematurely scaling prior to product/market fit.

Per a report from the Startup Genome Project, the number one cause of startup failure is premature scaling.[4] Startup Genome estimates that 74 percent of high-growth Internet startups fail due to *premature scaling*, which is defined as "focusing on one dimension of the business and advancing it out of sync with the rest of the operation." This happens when a startup expands too quickly, spends too much money on this expansion, and then finds revenue being outpaced by expenses. You can fall into the trap of premature scaling by overspending on customer acquisition, confusing early adopters with a larger market segment, or by shifting engineering resources out of R&D and into technical support too quickly.

Ponder this messy example:

Mrs. D. has invented a biodegradable toilet paper that degrades 10 times faster than all other toilet paper. She files a patent on her product, but before going to market to see if customers want her innovation, she decides to corner the market on her paper's key ingredient. Doing so costs her millions of dollars, but ensures she is the only one who can sell her product. A year later, she has cornered the market on the supply of highly biodegradable toilet paper. Unfortunately, Mrs. D. didn't conduct pilot tests or focus groups on her innovation with real customers. Thus, Mrs. D. was shocked to learn that end users don't like her product, so much so that her customers, primarily the large distributors of toilet paper, won't carry it since they already sell cheap nonbiodegradable toilet paper. Mrs. D. has prematurely scaled her business.

Reasonable Not Right

While predicting the future accurately is impossible, it doesn't stop many entrepreneurs from announcing that their five-year future revenue forecast is conservative. Many entrepreneurs misunderstand the motivation behind investors' interest in future results. Investors prefer reasonable to right. Since it is impossible to predict your revenue in five years, entrepreneurs should spend less time trying to prove their numbers are correct. Instead, founders should understand and be clear about the assumptions that lead to these numbers and include them in their plan.

Josh Brooks from Postcard on the Run illustrates what happens when you aren't reasonable. Postcard on the Run[5] allows its users to send personalized postcards from anywhere in the world. You simply take a picture, write a message, sign with your finger, and send it off, all done from the convenience of your mobile phone. Josh demonstrates several aspects of an effective pitch, but he does not show the ability to be reasonable when making his company's valuation proposal. He states that for $300,000, the Sharks can have 5 percent of his company (a $6 million valuation). Given the very early stage of Postcard on the Run, Josh isn't being reasonable, and the Sharks chew him up.

Melissa Carbone creates live horror attractions. She has run haunted hayrides in Los Angeles and New York as well as a haunted camping trip. Last year, her venture generated $1 million in gross sales. While this impressed the Sharks, they were unimpressed with her valuing her company at $20 million, along with her inability to articulate a rationale for the valuation. In the end, Mark Cuban and Carbone agreed to an investment of $2 million for 20 percent, making her post-money valuation a more reasonable $10 million.

THE ART OF FINANCIAL FORECASTING
By John Pinsent, Ca, ICD.D (St. Arnaud Pinsent Steman, Chartered Accountants)

Effective financial forecasting is an entrepreneur's business GPS. Financial forecasting allows entrepreneurs to know accurately and objectively where they are along the route to success, where they want to get to, and, most importantly, receive helpful instructions along the way. For first-time entrepreneurs, the task of creating financial statements and the financial model that underlies them is daunting. Having never walked this path before, entrepreneurs often barely know where the ON button is, let alone how to navigate to the nearly mythical exit that is their destination. Fortunately, many prior travelers on the road to startup success have walked this path before you, although many of these entrepreneurs have also gotten lost along the way. But if you keep to the basics and stay the course of best practices, then you, too, can learn to navigate the highway of effective financial forecasting.

As an angel investor, I'll consider your financial forecast the third most important thing as I'm contemplating my investment. First, I need to like you and your team. Can I trust you? Do you have the skills necessary to build a valuable enterprise? Next, I need to like your concept. Is it unique? Can I imagine people engaging with it and is it the kind of business that I would be proud to be associated with? Can I offer more than cash? Once you've cleared these two hurdles—team and idea—I turn my attention to your financial forecasts. Like team and idea, financial forecasts, while varied, can quickly help me make that all-important first decision: Do I want to hear more?

Why are financial forecasts so important? The simple answer is that the financial forecast tells investors a lot about you and your business. By reviewing your forecasts, we will learn a lot about your market, your margins, and your business mechanics. Through this analysis, we'll discover much of what investors need to know about how you are going to take my hard-earned money, and hopefully turn this great idea into a healthy profit for us all. But we learn more than just the numbers from your financials. We also learn the level of business acumen of your team. Business acumen ensures that the financials are realistic, achievable, and based on grounded real-life experience and reasonable assumptions. You don't have to be right, but you do have to be reasonable.

Your financial forecasts also serve to set the tone for how the investment is going to be valued and what an investor's expected rate of return will be. If your forecasts are far off the road of reality, then you've sent me a clear message that you don't understand your business, your market, or your ability to capture value from both. If your financial forecasts are excessively conservative, then you run the risk of losing my interest by failing to hit my return on investment expectations. After all, no one wants to put $50,000 into a high-risk venture if the upside is only 10 percent. Bill Gates often talks about how people overestimate what they will achieve in the short term and underestimate what they will realize over the long haul. He's absolutely right! The art of financial forecasting is finding that balance between operational realism and infectious entrepreneurial optimism.

If you want to impress a potential investor, I suggest you and all entrepreneurs keep the following things in mind as you develop your financial forecasts.

Anchor in the present: I'm going to intensely analyze the first year or any period that the current round of financing will cover. I'll be interested in knowing how years two and three are expected to play out, but will put anything beyond those years down to pure optimistic speculation. The key is to anchor in the present and scale from there (e.g., we are projecting $100,000 in the first year and are pushing to double that in each of the following years). Make sure the plan for the next year holds water.

(Continued)

(*Continued*)

Forget the exit: Unless you've built and sold a business several times before, I know that you don't have a clue about where this opportunity will take us. Don't be afraid to dream big, but know that the valuation for the purposes of my investment will rest on the details of the next 12 months.

Bottom-up, not top-down: Your financial forecasts should be tied to your operational realities. If you are projecting sales of $2 million, then the assumptions on which your financial forecast are built must include staffing, advertising, travel, and marketing budgets that can realistically expect to deliver that level of sales activity. If you have product engineering work to be done, then the number of project hours needed to complete that work must tie into a head count and related staffing budget that can deliver those hours. Ultimately, you'll be held accountable for how investment dollars are spent. What your financial forecast should show investors is that your business will include an accountability framework that will ensure that your targets can be achieved within the timelines and budget dollars you are projecting. Remember, no one expects you to be right, just reasonable.

Ask for directions: While all founders have different levels of financial acumen, they should ground their projections in reality. One way to do that is to ask for directions. Solicit input on your financials from those who have more experience than you. Test your assumptions with future clients, with potential suppliers, and with advisors. The more you test your assumptions and adjust based on third-party feedback, the more comfortable most investors will be.

Plan macro and execute micro: Investors understand that it is very difficult to accurately predict the path that the commercialization of your product will take. I need to see and understand the financial framework at a macro level. The details and assumptions below that level should give me the confidence that you've thought through all of those details and have a plan to execute at that micro level. If you win me over on the framework, I'll give you the rope to execute at the day-to-day level.

Fresh and evolved: Keep your forecasts fresh and your assumptions fluid. If your forecasts are for the current year and we're already in December, they don't have much value to me. Prepare your forecasts so that they can roll with your operational milestones as they are realized. Ensure that you can update your forecasts in real time to reflect operational realities, such as not being able to fill a key management role at the exact time you thought it would be filled. Generally, the software that you use to build your forecasts will allow for dynamic updates to assumptions and key input variables. Stay current with all the key data points. Remember, you will be expected to ground your financials in reality. If you miss your sales target, you can't simply reforecast it retroactively to address the issue. You must, instead, understand why the sales target was missed and adjust the assumptions in the financial model.

> As the investor, I want you to paint me a financial picture that captures my imagination and my pocketbook. Show me the road map of the investment highway that you wish us to drive down together. If you integrate your framework into realistic details to which you're prepared to be held accountable, then investors will have the basis on which they can comfortably move forward. In this turbulent economy, I want a comfortable ride to an awesome destination with a reliable driver. Investors are not afraid of getting lost, they're just afraid to drive with founders who won't stop to ask for directions.

Get Out of the Building

Many startups used to run in stealth mode until they launched their product. *Stealth mode* was the term used for "Sssssshhhhh, don't tell anyone what we are working on. If they know they will steal our idea."

The problem with this approach is internal bias. If the only information you are getting is coming from yourself, how can you validate this information? Steve Blank expresses the logic flaw as follows:

- An intelligent opinion is still a guess.
- The dumbest person with a fact trumps anyone with an opinion.
- There are no facts inside the building, so get the heck outside.

Getting out of the building is one of the key tenets of today's Lean Startup movement. It is based on the hypothesis that the value of customer feedback far outweighs the benefits of secrecy. Instead of building a solution confidentially in a garage for two years and then launching it to customers, you should launch your product early and often. By doing so, you can work directly with end users to shape the growth and value proposition of the solution. And you'll avoid mistakes made by only listening to the people you perceive as the smartest in your room. The rhetorical question becomes "If no business plan survives first contact with customers, when do you want first contact to occur? After you have built the product or before?"

In Techstars, one of the key activities during the 90-day accelerator program is to expose each company's product and ideas to a wide variety of mentors. During the first 30 days, an intense experience called *mentor whiplash* occurs. After the twentieth mentor meeting,

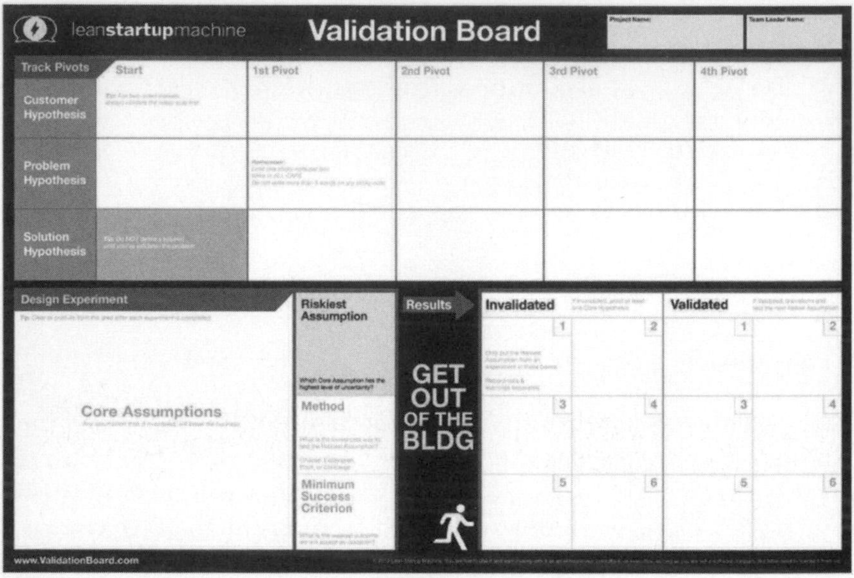

Figure 9.1   Validation Board

an entrepreneur realizes she has received a wide variety of advice, including suggestions that contradict each other. At the same time, the entrepreneur is told that what she is hearing is merely data—it's up to her to figure out what is valid, what is invalid, and what to do with it. By getting an avalanche of conflicting data early, the entrepreneur quickly realizes the value of collecting even more data as she searches for patterns to help hone the product.

Our friends at the Lean Startup machine have created a framework to assist new companies in getting out of the building. They call it the Validation Board and it can be used to ensure a founder stays laser focused (see Figure 9.1). The Validation Board forces entrepreneurs to validate their unique value proposition before building or coding their minimum viable product.

Plan B

In two decades of venture investing, we have never seen a business end up where it predicted it would. Things change and innovative things change quickly. As result, every opportunity needs a backup plan, a Plan B. In fact, have a Plan C and Plan D as well.

Ideally your product, solution, or service has multiple uses or user types. For example, billing software for law firms could probably also do well in accounting firms, but it might also be used for nonbilling purposes. Understanding the various opportunities for monetization is key at the evaluation stage.

Things change. Competitors appear. Governments repeal regulations. Key staff leave. Your ability to formulate multiple plans for when the first one doesn't work is a key characteristic of a great entrepreneur.

Founder's Perspective: Disqus
By Daniel Ha (Co-Founder)

We started Disqus because we cared about online communities. That is, the traditional understanding of online communities: message boards, forums, Usenet groups, and IRC channels. These are where the geeks and experts get together to share and learn from one another. That's different from social networks where people share with friends and family. Online communities, in our opinion, are at the core of what makes the Internet amazing. Disqus was started to explore how to unlock major value from this in a way that's never been done before.

Because the Disqus mission was personal to me, building the product and business was inherently an opportunity that I knew I could spend a lot of time pursuing. That makes it an opportunity worth considering.

To use Disqus, people install Disqus on their websites. That's all they should do to get going. This approach to online communities proved to be successful for us because it allowed Disqus to very quickly grow a network. In a relatively short time frame, the network spanned millions of websites and billions of page views.

But the business opportunity was not always obvious to us. Initially, it was all free to use. Would people pay for this? Are we building a software service company? We tried a variety of models and began to narrow down to a core hypothesis. This was done by paying attention to how people used our products as well as understanding what type of company it was that we wanted to build. Whatever business model we would end up pursuing, we knew that our opportunity was in a community network with unparalleled scale and reach. We knew that the company that we were building should have a revenue model that matched the ambitious scale of our product.

All of this is to basically say that we didn't have a true business plan at the very beginning. But because of the fast, sustained growth of our product's adoption, I knew that we were doing something interesting for a nontrivial number of people. The fact that it grew in the face of real competition meant that we were doing something right in our execution. Very early on, we outlined ways that Disqus could make revenue. It was important to consider a few different pathways,

(Continued)

(*Continued*)

knowing that if we were going to build a valuable company, we would eventually have multiple products with potentially multiple lines of revenue. So, the most important thing was to create a foundation that told us that we had true product/market fit.

The software-as-a-service model didn't work out for us. Not because there wasn't a market there; it was because building that type of business wasn't part of our core DNA. We didn't naturally do it well, and we didn't have much desire to try to do it well. If we continued, I realized that we'd be building a company that I didn't want to work on anymore. So we make a bold decision and abandoned this growing revenue line and completely shifted to another type of business: advertising and media. We knew that as a network with sufficient scale we had more than a product—we had an ecosystem that was valuable for many different parts of our market.

This was a more ambitious plan and one that's harder to execute. But it was an opportunity that supported the original mission and would help us create the company that we wanted to keep building.

Investor's Perspective: Disqus
By Naval Ravikant (Investor)

I met Daniel at Y Combinator Demo Day in late 2007. I'd been experimenting with viral growth applications at the time (it was still a relatively new framework back then), and I was impressed by how quickly communities could be built online. I chatted with Daniel about it at YC Demo Day, and he struck me as quiet and competent.

Daniel was extremely professional—he followed up and smartly asked me for advice rather than for money. I went to see them in their apartment/office. It's striking how bad the state of blog commenting was back then. The Disqus product was lightyears ahead of the native commenting systems. I was personally using Squarespace at the time and as a nascent blogger, I felt the pain. I also have a strong belief that every product is better when it's made social. The promise of the web isn't to connect people to computers but rather through computers.

Daniel kept updating me month by month on the stats—never pushing or chasing, but not being silent either. That built trust quickly. It also helped that the team was iterating their product quickly, and growing. They went from 1 million page views a month in October to 20 million in November to 35 million in December. Clearly, they were on to something.

The hard part with a product like Disqus is monetization. The scale required before you can monetize a conversational social app is enormous, so that was a big leap of faith to make. Regardless, communities are sticky and have huge value and it was clear that the blogosphere was growing, and Disqus even more so. At the end of the day, I made the bet that a huge, diffuse community would still have value down the road and that Disqus could aggregate enough attention that advertisers would care. I made a few other similar bets that year. Most failed, but luckily, Twitter and Disqus did not.

I did a due diligence call with Fred Wilson, who was also looking at the deal. I was so impressed by the team that I offered the group an independent term sheet but eventually ended up hitching a ride on Fred's investment.

Daniel never did get much value out of me on the viral marketing side. He didn't need it—the product inherently markets itself, and like at all the best companies, like those at all the best companies, Disqus' entrepreneurs had great instincts and didn't need this investor much.

Notes

1. Steve Blank, "No Business Plan Survives First Contact with a Customer—The 5.2 Billion Dollar Mistake," Steve Blank's blog, November 1, 2010, http://steveblank.com/2010/11/01/no-business-plan-survives-first-contact-with-a-customer-%E2%80%93-the-5-2-billion-dollar-mistake/ and "No Plan Survives First Contact with Customers—Business Plans versus Business Models," Steve Blank's blog, April 8, 2010, https://steveblank.com/2010/04/08/no-plan-survives-first-contact-with-customers-%E2%80%93-business-plans-versus-business-models/.
2. Reproduced with permission from David Cohen, "Launch Early and Often," *Wall Street Journal*, Accelerators, July 29, 2013, http://blogs.wsj.com/accelerators/2013/07/29/david-cohen-launch-early-and-often/.
3. David Cohen and Brad Feld, *Do More Faster* (Hoboken, NJ: John Wiley & Sons, 2011), 20.
4. "Summary of Startup Genome Report Extra: Premature Scaling," Compass blog, April 2, 2013, http://blog.startupcompass.co/pages/summary-of-startup-genome-report-extra-premat.
5. *Shark Tank*: Season 5, Episode 1.

CHAPTER 10

Pitch

The pitch refers to both the written and oral presentation of your business. Many investors see a causal link between the ability to pitch and the potential success of the company. Some investors even believe that founders who can't pitch are doomed, because without the ability to convince others of the merit of your business, you will struggle to attract investors, employees, partners, and customers.

The shortest version of the pitch is known as the elevator pitch. This is a minute-long summary of the business that can be delivered during a typical elevator ride of 20 floors. The elevator pitch covers two topics: What do you do and why should I care? A great entrepreneur can deliver it without it feeling memorized or stiff. The goal of the elevator pitch is for the audience to be intrigued enough to want to learn more about your business.

Regardless of the task at hand, you need a good elevator pitch. Want to raise capital? You need to pitch your business. Want to attract top-notch employees? You need to pitch your vision. Want to attract strategic partners? You need to pitch the benefits of working together. Want to increase sales? You need to pitch your solution. The elevator pitch describes the pain your company is feeling and the way your product addresses this pain. The pain statement clearly outlines the need for the product and includes some sense of market size.

A good elevator pitch has four characteristics. It is:

1. *Concise*: More than one minute is too long.
2. *Clear*: No jargon allowed.
3. *Compelling*: Induces greed.
4. *Irrefutable*: The statements are hard to deny.

The following is an example of an elevator pitch for eBay:

One person's trash is another person's treasure. Our online garage sale brings together buyers and sellers from around the world. Some are looking to sell what they consider trash. Others want to buy what they consider to be treasure.

Creating an emotional connection between your product and your audience is the best way to motivate the consumer to buy. For example, the ShamWow pitch to customers—"ShamWow washes, dries, and polishes any surface. It's like a towel, chamois, and sponge all in one!"—calls to mind that annoying feeling someone gets when cleaning up a big spill with standard paper towels.

Catherine Langin pitched the Miner's Lunchbox,[1] which has been available for sale for over 50 years. By sharing the rich history of her product and the inventor Leo May, she could induce a feeling of nostalgia. After she confirmed they had made money in the past, one investor proclaimed, "I love the story, but I love to hear that you made money." Catherine then explained, "Leo May has sold over one million lunch boxes." As soon as she said that, the Dragons felt their greed kick in and understood the Miner's Lunchbox was an investment that could make them money.

Short Form (Under 10 Minutes)

While the elevator pitch typically lasts a minute, once you are successful and are invited to talk more about your business, you need a longer version of your elevator pitch. This short version, which should last between 5 and 10 minutes, goes deeper into what you are doing and should include sections on the problem, solution, target market, competition, team, a financial summary, and the milestones you are going to achieve.

Long Form (30 Minutes)

The long form of the elevator pitch is the investor presentation. Much has been written about the investor presentation, but one of our favorite sets of guidelines comes from Guy Kawasaki, who suggests that all pitches follow the 10/20/30 PowerPoint rule:[2]

- No smaller than 30-point font
- No longer than 20 minutes
- No more than 10 slides

This may sound easy, but it's not. By limiting yourself to 10 slides, you end up focusing on the high-level issues. By pumping up the font size, you ensure that the slides provide overarching themes rather than extensive detail. By limiting time, you ensure that you save some for discussion.

The 10 slides can vary, but a good framework consists of the following:

1. *The problem*: Whose problem is it? How big a problem is this? What is the status quo?
2. *Your solution*: How is your solution 10× better than what exists? Scalable? Proprietary? Better than the status quo?
3. *Business Model*: Who pays whom? Who are the users? Who are the paying customers?
4. *Underlying technology*: What intellectual property is your product based on? Where did it come from?
5. *Marketing and sales*: How will you attract users? What is the cost of client acquisition?
6. *Competition*: Who else is doing this? How are you different? Why will you crush them?
7. *Team*: Who is in your Talent Triangle? Who has business acumen? Domain knowledge? Operational experience?
8. *Projections and milestones*: How will you use the proceeds? What key moments are upcoming?
9. *Status and timeline*: What have you accomplished to date? When and what is the next value inflection point?
10. *Summary and call to action*: How much are you raising? How does this fit with the investor's investment thesis, current portfolio, and recent investments? Why are you the next opportunity to back?

Business Plan—or Not

Prior to the dot-com boom, a business plan was considered a required document for raising money. Around 1999, when the boom was in full swing, the business plan fell out of favor and millions of dollars were raised just based on an outline of a plan, which was often shared as a PowerPoint presentation. Most business plans, or outlines of plans, followed a similar template that highlighted nine key sections:

1. Company summary
2. Market
3. Problem/opportunity
4. Solution/product
5. Business model
6. Team
7. Go-to-market plan
8. Milestones/metrics
9. Financial projections

Remember that business plans never survive first contact with the customer. As a result, the business plan is obsolete the moment the entrepreneur starts to implement it. Historically, entrepreneurs would spend hundreds of hours on a business plan that might not even be read and would certainly evolve.

Today, business plans have been replaced with a concept based on the Business Model Canvas, originally created by Alexander Osterwalder and Yves Pigneur in their book, *Business Model Generation*.[3] The Lean Canvas is a version of the Business Model Canvas used by many startups.

The Lean Canvas presents the core assumptions for each of the nine main elements of a business in a visual manner, highlighting:

1. Problem
2. Customer segments
3. Unique value proposition
4. Solution
5. Channels
6. Cost structure
7. Revenue streams
8. Key metrics
9. Unfair advantage

Unlike the business plan, which is meant to be updated on a periodic basis, the Business Model Canvas gets updated daily. The goal of the founders is to go through each assumption in the canvas and confirm or reject this assumption based on actual interactions with potential customers through customer development. Thus, the Business Model Canvas is a living, evolving, modern-day version of the business plan.

Executive Summary

Another document that entrepreneurs should arm themselves with is the executive summary. This is a one- to three-page summary of the key elements of your business that uses a paragraph to summarize each section of a traditional business plan. It should be an easy-to-consume document that is focused on being reasonable rather than right. The purpose, beyond describing the overview of the business, is to show readers that the founders are knowledgeable, informed, and rational in their choices.

Q&A

While most interactions with a potential investor around a new business usually begin with an elevator pitch, they almost always end with questions being asked. The best investors aren't only listening to the answers, but are observing how the answers are being given. Has the entrepreneur thought through the question or has she simply given a canned answer? Does she get frustrated? Do all team members presenting get involved? Do each of the founders give the same answers? If an investor disagrees with the answer and pushes back on the response, how does the entrepreneur react?

As discussed in the earlier sections on coaching and mentorship, exploring an idea is a dynamic process, one in which many mistakes will be made. How an entrepreneur interacts during Q&A can often shed light on the founders' business approach. Some entrepreneurs see questions as a way of exploring deeper topics of interest that the audience wishes to learn more about. Other entrepreneurs see questions as an attack on the opportunity. The former is ideal—the latter, not so much.

Founder's Perspective: Next Big Sound
By Alex White (Co-Founder)

Going back to the early pitch, why was Next Big Sound a great opportunity? We had several factors working in our favor. First, we were positioned in a sexy, multibillion-dollar global industry. We found ourselves amid a massive, well-documented disruption in the way people consume music. We faced a large, but

(Continued)

(*Continued*)

slow, incumbent player in Nielsen SoundScan. There was general confusion in the marketplace about which numbers were worth tracking and how the music industry should navigate the digital world.

I wish that I could say that our pitch came down from the mountaintop fully written, but that is pretty much the opposite of what happened.

We started in the summer of 2009 with several different ideas for the company we could build. Most of the ideas revolved around the music industry, and I had standing weekly calls with a dozen band managers to bounce ideas off as we went about validating which ideas we should pursue. One of the key questions I made sure to ask was "Would this be valuable enough for you to pay for?" That screened out a lot of fun, early ideas that we never could monetize. We had tried building a consumer app the year prior and were about to shut down the company when we were accepted into Techstars. This time, we swore we would build something that could generate revenue from day one without having to get a million users first.

The managers we talked to were going around to every site where their artist had a presence and noting the number of new plays, views, fans, and comments in Excel spreadsheets. They, or their assistants, would do this Monday through Friday, and chart growth on a daily and weekly basis. They would skip the weekends, miss days, not collect it at the same time each day, and generally spend all their time collecting the numbers instead of analyzing and making sense of them.

That's when we presented them with our software that could automatically collect this data daily and allow them to export the information to Excel. They would then be able to compare this data to that of any other artist in the world and cross-reference it with concert and event data for full context. We had hundreds of conversations with managers, labels, agents, and others who were trying to collect and analyze this data by hand.

In my conversations at the beginning of the summer, not one of these managers said, "Hey, you should track online data and provide a centralized dashboard to see everything going on with my artists." It was only after I showed them that we were doing that that they started to say, "Wow, you would save me many hours of work each week if you could track data for my whole roster!"

It was the first idea we struck on where potential customers were already taking time-consuming and painful measures to solve the problem on their own. We knew we were onto something when we kept hearing the same thing repeatedly from individual artists up to the biggest managers and labels in the world.

Investor's Perspective: Next Big Sound
By Jason Mendelson (Foundry Group)

It didn't take me long to realize that Next Big Sound was a great investment opportunity, which is somewhat ironic given that I wasn't sold on the idea at first. But I was instantly sold on the team. The pitch was as much about the people, their passion, and the problem they knew they wanted to solve, even if they didn't have the final answer. The pitch was that the founding team was, while young, broad in experience and deep in commitment to not only the industry but to one another as partners. They were smart and self-aware.

While normally an uninteresting idea causes me to think about other opportunities, I couldn't let this team off so easily. They quickly came up with their killer idea. The early pitch was simple to understand yet emotionally powerful: Like baseball in the old days, the music industry is run by instinct, luck, and long-held superstitions, and that is putting it generously. The time for hard data is now, especially considering the "moneyball" success in sports. Knowing that I was and am a musician, they pitched right to my emotions. Thus, I felt an emotional connection to the problem and intellectually knew that technology had become viable to provide unprecedented insights into the industry. This became Next Big Sound.

We had invested in the music industry previously. My Foundry Group partner, Ryan McIntyre, and I had spent countless hours, and beers, discussing the future of the music industry. What Ryan and I had assumed, however, was that information was ubiquitous. After listening to the NBS team, it was clear that we had assumed wrong. What NBS pitched was that for any change to happen in the industry, facts, not opinions, must be known, and they would be the team to unearth, discover, digest, and provide insights around these facts. They also proved to me that most of the needed information was in the public domain, not stuck behind a pay-walled proprietary database. They showed me incredible screenshots of what they would build that convinced me they could deliver a ton of information in a clear and concise manner.

They then explained in plain English the technical architecture, their assumptions around the costs to provide the service, and what they thought they could charge for it. One of the unique things they discussed with me was why their potential customers might hate their product. It was this discussion, which was honest, insightful, and transparent, that led me to believe they had a handle on most of the major growth issues even before they got a start.

In the end, we invested because they were doing all the regular startup stuff: They were attacking a big market that was ready for change, had a great team, and a solid business model. Where they stood out was their transparency, willingness to learn, and a pitch that answered just about every question that I had going into the presentation. While they hadn't built a ton of code at the time, what they had built was beautiful. But the sheer amount of data they had about what they were going to do coupled with the convictions and opinions that would run the business were way ahead of most companies I see at that stage.

Notes

1. *Dragons' Den*: Season 4, Episode 3.
2. Guy Kawasaki, "The 10/20/30 Rule of Power Point," *How to Change the World*, December 30, 2005, https://guykawasaki.com/the_102030_rule/.
3. Alexander Osterwalder and Yves Pigneur, *Business Model Generation: A Handbook for Visionaries, Game Changers, and Challengers* (Hoboken, NJ: John Wiley & Sons, 2010).

CHAPTER

11

Raising Money

Your need for capital can have a big impact on your opportunity. While we touch on fundraising briefly in this chapter, a much more comprehensive book on this topic is *Venture Deals: Be Smarter Than Your Lawyer and Venture Capitalist* by Brad and his partner Jason Mendelson.

The Timmons Model of the Entrepreneurial Process[1] lists resources as the third pillar of the startup process (see Figure 11.1). While resources cover more than just capital, capital for investment is often one of the most sought after.

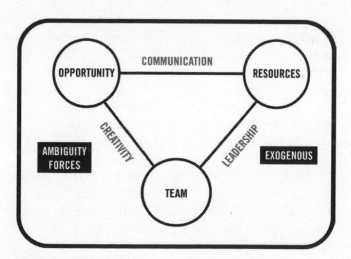

Figure 11.1   The Entrepreneurial Process

Source: The Timmons Model, J. A. Timmons and S. Spinelli (1999).

125

Recognize that many companies raise little to no outside capital. Brad's first company, Feld Technologies, only raised $10, which was used to allocate the stock among the three founders (Brad, his partner Dave Jilk, and his father Stan Feld, who was an advisor to Brad and Dave). In many cases, you'll be able to build a successful company without any meaningful outside capital. In others, you need capital to get going and fuel your growth.

Raising capital has a secondary benefit beyond money, namely, the signal it sends to the market. If you recall the discussion on signaling theory, having experienced angels or venture capitalists (VCs) invest in your company can generate a strong halo effect. Consider the halo effect that a famous entrepreneur, such as Google's Eric Schmidt, would impart to your new startup if he invested. Or how a strategic investment from Cisco Systems could validate the new collaboration software you are working on.

Building a Relationship with a Potential Investor

Relationships with investors are hard to develop and often take a long time. A good analogy is that you can bring the same dynamic to building your relationship with an investor that you do when dating. When you are introduced to someone, you don't immediately ask them to marry you. Rather, you start with a first date, hopefully followed by more dates. Over time, you develop a relationship that either evolves into something beautiful or tails off and ends. Let your relationship with an investor evolve the same way.

Techstars Boulder Managing Director Nicole Glaros has a great mantra, which is that "If you want money, ask for advice."[2] Rather than approach your relationship with the investor as one where you are focused only on asking for money, take the opposite tack and ask for advice. Don't be generic about it—understand what the investor knows and has experience with, and start the relationship by approaching it with questions, rather than answers.

Explore what you can do for the investor, rather than what the investor can do for you. Fred Wilson, a VC who has an extremely popular blog, says that the best way for someone he doesn't know to get his attention is to engage with his VC community, comment on his posts, and interact regularly through this mechanism as a way of getting to know him. Mark Suster, another popular VC blogger, talks about how he loves to invest in lines, not dots.[3]

Remember, you are building a relationship. Take your time and do it the way the investor wants to do it rather than with an aggressive, generic approach.

Who Makes the Ask?

Hi. My name is Bob, from Buffalo. Our company, BuffaloWingz, solves the problem of hot sauce on your keyboard. We are looking for $50,000 for 5 percent of our company.

Sound familiar? This is how most pitches on *Shark Tank* and *Dragons' Den* begin. But this is almost always exactly the opposite of what should happen.

When raising money for your company, the investors generally set the price. While the entrepreneur should have an opinion on the company's potential valuation, she shouldn't disclose it in the first few minutes of a discussion with a prospective investor.

Always remember that your company's valuation is negotiable. The valuation is a contractual term, negotiated by the parties involved. It is not set by formula, nor is it based on a single explicit parameter, such as your company's revenue. The price an investor is willing to pay is influenced by that investor's recent funding history, the current market valuation for similar companies, and the stage of your business. Most important, if you have multiple investors interested in your company, you'll have more leverage on the valuation.

Investors, especially venture capitalists, often want to own enough of the company to make the investment material to them. But at the same time, investors also want to ensure that the founders maintain a large enough stake in the business to be rewarded for their entrepreneurial efforts.

Use of Proceeds

The use of proceeds is what you are going to do with the money. When discussing the use of proceeds, you should include both the actions you are going to undertake with the money, such as hiring three Bay Area–based salespeople, as well as what these actions will result in, such as generating an additional $2 million of annual recurring revenue. Once you've begun to engage with an investor, make sure you talk openly about what success means and how you are going to measure it.

Katrina Mijares pitched Toddlerobics[4] and was asked by investors why she needed to raise money. Her response was "It will cover the market research and advertising development" to establish her product as a brand. This didn't please investors, who responded, "You haven't come to the table with a process to establish that brand. I hear no steps; there's no branding." Compare that to the response Trevor Bielby of Schmotoboard[5] gave those same investors, which was "to build up inventory, to put 100 of these on the floor. I have stores in Calgary willing to sell them. I plan to outsource, but with friends; we can make 100 a week." Bielby was specific about why he needed to raise money, while Mijares wasn't.

Like all financial forecasts based on future action, it is only important to investors that founders be reasonable, not right. No one expects you to accurately know the sales figures for new hires, but they do want to know that the cost of those new hires over a particular time period is smaller than the amount being raised.

Raise the Least Amount of Money to Get to the Next Level

Determining how much to ask from investors is tricky. Ask for too little and you risk running out of capital before reaching your goals. Ask for too much and you may give away too much equity too early or scare off potential investors with an unrealistic ask.

We are often asked how much money entrepreneurs should attempt to raise. We believe the amount you should raise is the least amount of money you need to make it to the next level of your business. As the entrepreneur, you get to define each of these terms, both the least amount of money you need as well as what the next level is. Then, add a buffer of between three and six more months. Your goal is to not need to raise more money until well after you are at the next value inflection point in your business.

A value inflection point occurs when you reach a set of milestones that increase the value of your business while mitigating risk. These are baby steps on the road to success. Common value inflection points include:

- Launching a product
- Selling to your first customers
- Converting pilots to recurring customers

- Achieving breakeven revenue vs. expenses
- Successfully launching into a second market

Another approach to determining the amount of capital raised is based on Hofstadter's Law,[6] which states that most projects will cost three times as much and take twice as long to hit their goals as projected.

Let X be the amount being raised, in dollars.

Let B be the monthly burn rate (i.e., how much it costs to run the company each month).

Let Y be the next value inflection point (i.e., the next major milestone to be hit).

Let T be the number of months that it will take, post-funding to hit Y.

The formula that results is: $X = 2T(B)$.

A startup burning $10,000 a month that is six months away from hitting its breakeven point should seek $120,000 in investment $(X = 2(6)(\$10,000))$.

Instead of looking at this as a universal law, use it as a starting point for approximating what you should be raising. Ultimately, you should ensure you have enough time and money to reach your next value inflection point while including a cushion to account for the vagaries of building a startup. Remember that the only thing certain in all startups is the high level of uncertainty involved.

Ask for Money from the Right Kind of Investor

Different investors invest in different stages of a company. If you are at the very beginning of your journey, start with angels, friends, and family. Once you've got a product in the market and have some momentum, approach early-stage VCs. Do your research in advance and make sure the investor you are approaching invests in your company's type and stage.

Cameron's Spectrum of Financing (see Figure 11.2) dates to the 1990s, when it took millions of dollars to bring a product to market. Today, the cost of bringing a product to market has dropped

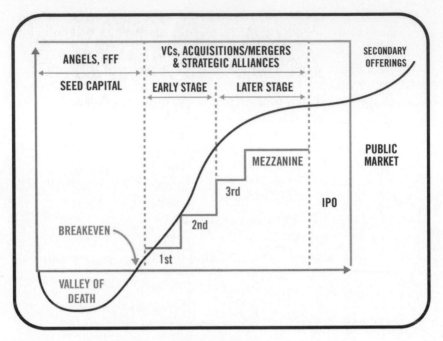

Figure 11.2   Cameron's (1998) Spectrum of Financing[7]

dramatically and methodologies like the Lean Startup help an entrepreneur make dramatic progress with substantially less capital. So how do these changes impact the funding cycle for startups? Compare Cameron's model, which originates from the T. A. Pai Management Institute in 1998 with Tony Bailetti and Sonia Bot's (2013) revised model shown in Figure 11.3.

In the late 1990s, VCs poured millions into ventures without revenue, traction, or even a proven business model. Now, two decades later, VCs generally invest in either companies with a proven and scalable business model or entrepreneurs they have worked with before who have achieved this in their previous company.

Today, seed funding is about getting a minimum viable product (MVP) built and discovering product/market fit. This is very different from 20 years ago, when the first round of VC funding generally went to building and launching the product in the first place.

In addition to investing in different stages, investors focus on specific industries, industry segments, types of companies, and geographies. An investor who typically invests in business-to-business SaaS companies is unlikely to invest in a natural foods company.

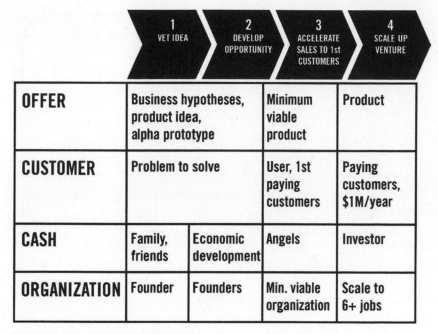

	1 VET IDEA		2 DEVELOP OPPORTUNITY	3 ACCELERATE SALES TO 1st CUSTOMERS	4 SCALE UP VENTURE
OFFER	Business hypotheses, product idea, alpha prototype			Minimum viable product	Product
CUSTOMER	Problem to solve			User, 1st paying customers	Paying customers, $1M/year
CASH	Family, friends	Economic development		Angels	Investor
ORGANIZATION	Founder	Founders		Min. viable organization	Scale to 6+ jobs

Figure 11.3   Lead to Win Lifecycle Stage Model

Source: Tony Bailetti and Sonia Bot, *Spectrum of Finance for Lean Startups* (2013).[8]

An investor who limits his investing to the Pacific Northwest is unlikely to invest in a company in New York City.

Not all investors are created equal. Investors with valuable corporate connections—who can participate in follow-on rounds or whose participation raises other investors' confidence—are generally more valuable than investors who only bring cash to the table. Investors' reputations, especially VCs', used to be very opaque and difficult to determine. With today's world of always-connected social media, it's much easier to understand an investor's preferences and behaviors. Unless you only have one choice for an investor, do your homework on them just like they are doing their due diligence on you.

Raise Money When It's Available

Today, some companies are raising massive funding rounds well before they need it. While this contradicts the idea of raising the least amount of money to get to the next level, it's simply a counterbalancing dynamic because of market conditions. Currently, the supply of early-stage capital seeking great opportunities far outweighs the demand. This isn't always the case and varies dramatically by stage, sector, geography, and timing.

In general, it's relatively easy to raise early-stage and late-stage capital but hard to raise mid-stage capital. In geographies that have healthy startup communities,[9] there is often a vibrant early-stage investor scene. This consists of experienced entrepreneurs who have cashed out of at least one business and are now reinvesting in new companies, along with early-stage VCs and other wealthy individuals who are drawn to investing locally. If you start a company in a city like Boulder, Colorado, raising your first $1 million is straight-forward.

If you have a successful business, have crossed through multiple inflection points, and are growing significantly, it'll be relatively easy for you to raise late-stage capital. Institutional investors, such as late-stage VCs and private equity firms, who want to invest $20 million or more, don't care where you are located. Late-stage money travels to opportunities.

Funding in the middle—between the first $1 million and the last $20 million—is always difficult to acquire, regardless of where you are in the cycle. This is the "prove it to me" zone where you have made some progress but haven't yet gotten to the point where you have an undeniably successful business.

Be opportunistic. But recognize there are cycles. It's easy today, but it will be hard again; you just don't know when.

You Aren't an Exception

When a professional investor raises a venture fund, he does so based on an investment thesis. One of the most successful funds of the last decade, Union Square Ventures, famously defined a future of valuable, new companies based on the principles of a network, summarized as "Large networks of engaged users, differentiated through user experience, and defensible through network effects."[10]

By defining what they invest in, investors stake out their territory. In some cases, the investment thesis may even be crystallized into a set of rules, such as:

- We will only invest in startups created under Canadian or American law.

- We will only invest in startups in the domain of the Internet of Things.
- We will only invest in scalable startups.
- We will only invest in startups that have proven their model and have revenue greater than $1 million.
- We will only invest in startups that have the potential to exit within five years.

While most VC firms publicize their investment thesis on their websites, many founders fail to research and respect the goals of these investors. We see this all the time—when restaurants apply to Techstars or when professional service firms complain about the lack of capital available to them.

Don't deceive yourself by thinking you are an exception to a VC firm's strategy. Before you approach VCs, do some research. There is no point in asking for seed money from a late-stage investor. If you are unsure of the investor's investment thesis or focus, simply investigate the last five companies she invested in to determine what these investments had in common. Spend more time researching the investors you are pitching and less time pitching investors.

Many entrepreneurs see an investment as extrinsic validation. It could be proof that the founder's crazy idea is worth pursuing, all the long hours invested by the entrepreneur were worth it, or that the road to riches is just around the corner. They couldn't be more wrong. While an investment can lead to the halo effect, receiving funding should not, in and of itself, be an endpoint. Too many founders see closing a financing round as a badge of honor, not a signal that the hard work is about to begin. Raising capital should be seen more akin to filling up your car with gas, a necessary and expensive evil. Once you've switched from bootstrapping to raising money, you have a new set of responsibilities to your investors. Most founders think the key to fundraising is quantity of their pitches, where the more they pitch, the more likely it is that they will raise money. This is generally wrong; quality dramatically trumps quantity. Instead of investing 100 hours to make 50 pitches, the wise founder investors 100 hours to make five pitches. The majority of that time should be conducting due diligence on potential investors, understanding who will be a good fit for them, and why. There is no point in pitching a mobile telco investor on a biotech deal. Likewise, there is no point in pitching a clean tech angel on gambling software. Matching your company to the startup thesis of the potential investor is a key premeeting activity. Giving the same investor pitch over and over is not. Spend less time pitching and more time researching and building a foundation for the relationship.

Why Anything Other Than a Yes Is a No

Even when you have found the ideal investor and have finally gotten a meeting, this is only the beginning of the process. Remember, while this may be your only investor target, you are not your potential investor's only choice. The demand for VC funding far exceeds the supply of smart money. The investor benchmarks are:

- For every 1,000 plans you see, you meet with fewer than 100.
- For every 100 companies you meet with, you will only perform due diligence on 5.
- For every five companies you do due diligence on, you will only invest in one.

A well-known East Coast investment fund looked at 3,000 companies last year, but only invested in a dozen companies. Similarly, a well-known Bay Area investor received over 10,000 inquiries last year, yet only made 10 investments. A typical Techstars program receives more than 1,000 applications for 10 slots. In general, the investor screening funnel looks a lot like the one in Figure 11.4.

Because of this math, VCs fund less than 1 percent of the pitches they hear, saying no hundreds or thousands of times a year. However, entrepreneurs often don't hear the word *no*. Instead, they hear statements like:

- If you find a lead investor, we might be interested in joining the round.
- I like it, but my partners don't.
- We will be interested once you have more traction.

Each of these comments is a different version of no, just said in veiled language. But even hearing this much is pleasant for

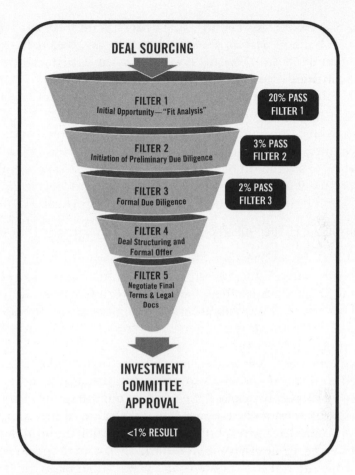

Figure 11.4   Investor Screening Funnel

entrepreneurs, because most investors fail to say anything at all. Instead, they just stop responding or slow down the dialogue. There are a few reasons why many investors don't say no explicitly, including:

The Option Excuse: Investors want to leave open the option to invest later, believing that at some future date, they may wish to get in.

The Missed Deal Excuse: Investors don't want to be the firm that should admit to passing on what became a successful company.[11]

The Bad Guy Excuse. The investor doesn't want to be the bad guy. He believes that no matter the reason he gives, the entrepreneurs will say, "You just don't get it," and he doesn't want to continue investing time in the dialogue.

Not all investors avoid saying no. Brad tries to say no to everything in under a minute.[12] He and many other VCs blog about what they are interested in and why they pass. Some investors even hold themselves to a standard of giving direct feedback to every entrepreneur they meet with.

Be Realistic about Your Valuation

A private company can be valued many ways, but ultimately it is entirely subjective. While investors often evaluate several key factors to decide at what price a deal makes sense to them, valuation is also about how much equity you are willing to give up and the potential returns the investment might generate. So, how do investors decide what a company is worth?

Fundamentally, they make it up, basing their view on the money invested to date, the potential returns, the risk associated with the business, the current state of the market, competition on the deal, and their decades of experience. The true value of the company is only known and set when both the investor and the entrepreneur come to an agreement on the number.

During the dot-com boom, page views (how many times users go to your website) were indicators of potential value. During the Web 2.0 boom (2003–2007), the number of registered users became the metric of choice. In the aftermath of the financial crisis (2008–2009), revenue and EBITDA made a comeback.

To further complicate matters, a decade ago $5 million was necessary to get a product to market. In 2010, that number dropped to $50,000. With such a low capital requirement, many investors, especially at the early stages, have shrugged off setting valuations and instead are investing using convertible debt, which becomes equity in the next financing round, often at a discount to the price the next round investors pay.

An entrepreneur pitched the Pizza Pak,[13] a plastic pizza case that would replace cardboard boxes, to a group of investors that included international pizza magnate Jim Treliving (chair of Boston Pizza). The entrepreneur valued his company at $1 million, yet he had not sold a single Pizza Pak. The founder claimed that his product would revolutionize the pizza industry without providing any proof of sales or customer testimonials. Even after Treliving shared his expert opinion that the Pizza Pak would not work, the entrepreneur persisted with this idea, anyway. The inflated valuation, the unsupported claims, and the blind insistence that he knew the pizza industry better than Jim Treliving only lowered his level of credibility.

Even Angels Have Investment Committees

Is raising money from angels easier than from VCs? You might think that it is since angels are usually high net worth individuals who are investing their own capital. Furthermore, most VCs invest many millions of dollars per company, whereas the average angel investment is in the hundreds of thousands.

The reality, however, is not that simple. Unlike most VCs, angels are investing their own hard-earned cash, and it's often the case that investing your own money brings a higher level of scrutiny than investing other people's money. Next, unlike VCs, the investment committee for an angel isn't made up of experienced private-equity professionals meeting at a board table. Instead, it is often made up of spouses meeting at the dining table. Angels typically don't have support infrastructure, such as analysts and associates, to support the transaction. Finally, many angels haven't seen dozens of term sheets, let alone negotiated them. Thus, angel investments often take as much time and energy as VC investments.

This, too, is changing. With innovations like AngelList, angel investing is being democratized and opened up to many more companies and investors.

The following founder/investor example from 3D Robotics provides a good soup-to-nuts example of taking an idea from serendipitous discovery to mere idea to MVP to full-blown product and on to a large, institutional fundraising effort. The confluence of the right founding team with the right domain expertise and the right (read: large and nascent) market with proven demand meant that once the founder reached out to the right investor, it didn't take long for the investment to follow.

Founder's Perspective: 3D Robotics
By Chris Anderson (Founder)

Step One: Do an Experiment, Get Mind Blown

It's 2007 and I'm editor of *Wired* magazine, with five young kids at home and a mission to bring the geek out in them (note: total failure so far). I notice that among the products that have arrived for review at the office one Friday are two boxes—one, the new Lego Mindstorms NXT robotics kit and the other, a radio-controlled (RC) airplane. I grab them both, promising to write a review, and plan a great GeekDad weekend: make a robot on Saturday and fly a plane on Sunday.

On Saturday, we dutifully build the Lego robots, which the kids promptly decide are stupid—they mostly roll slowly around and sometimes avoid walls. (They've seen Transformers—where are the frickin' lasers?) On Sunday, their main take-home lesson is that flying an RC plane is hard: It ends up in a tree, which I awkwardly climb, mortifying the kids and confirming their suspicions that geeky projects with Dad are always to be avoided.

In a desperate attempt to salvage what I could from the weekend, I tried to think how this could have gone better. What would have been a cooler robot and a better-flying plane? It suddenly occurred to me to simply combine the two boxes—get the Lego Mindstorms to fly the plane! I Googled *flying robot*, which led me to *drone*, which led me to *autopilot*, which led me to a lot of math that I didn't understand and ignored.

What I did learn is that a computer, sensors, and some code (pretty much what was in the Lego box) could fly a plane. I summoned the kids for one last session around the dining room table, and a couple hours later we had what I think was the world's first Lego Autopilot. We put it in the airplane, took it to the park, and although it didn't fly well, it did at least fly. (That first Lego drone is now in the Lego Museum in Billund, Denmark.)

The kids promptly lost interest and returned to video games, but the whole experience left me stunned. How was it possible that a dad and his kids could use Lego to build what I learned was technology regulated as a cruise missile controller? I felt that I'd suddenly glimpsed the future, much as I had when I'd tried my first web browser 15 years earlier. Something had changed in the world that made our dining-table invention possible—but what?

Step Two: Launch a Community to See Where This Goes

One thing that's always worked well for me is to ask stupid questions in public. It does two magical things: First, people answer my questions, and second, it encourages other people to ask their own stupid questions. Along the way, everybody gets smarter. So, I set up a simple social network to do just this—understand and build on my first Lego experiment—and called it DIY Drones. It quickly hit critical mass. Lots of other people were thinking about the same things I was right then, thanks to the new availability of cheap chip-based sensors and easy-to-use hardware hacking platforms such as Arduino. Soon, tens of thousands of people were starting to experiment with the new technology, much as the Homebrew Computing Club had done with the first cheap computer chips three decades earlier.

Step Three: Once Community Takes Off, Serve It

As the DIY Drones community grew, members started collaborating on software, electronics, and aircraft design, trading files and instructions on how to build home drones—that is, assuming you knew how to solder, compile code, and navigate complex directions written by engineers. But many of the newer members didn't want to do any of that hard stuff. They just wanted to buy a drone, ready to go, or at least a kit for an autopilot to control one. It became clear that someone would have to start a company to make and sell that. That someone might as well be me, at least as a sideline. I created 3D Robotics, a grand name for a weekend hobby. Our first assembly line was my kids packing baggies of parts into pizza boxes for an autonomous blimp kit (lesson: don't put a six-year-old on quality control).

Step Four: Get Lucky with Co-Founder

The hard part of the early autopilot kits was soldering and loading code on the circuit boards, which I quickly found was no way to spend a weekend. I needed a partner, and I asked the smartest guy on DIY Drones to join me. This was Jordi Munoz, who had been posting videos and code on how to control a toy helicopter with Arduino and a Wii controller. It was 2009, and he had just moved to Los Angeles from Tijuana, Mexico, and was bursting with ideas. He started soldering boards in his garage, then moved to an industrial shed. Then he moved to San Diego and rented an office and started hiring people and buying used manufacturing equipment, such as pick-and-place machines, on eBay. He downloaded the manuals from the Internet and taught himself to use them. A year later, we had a real factory, on little more than cash flow and just-do-it courage.

Step Five: Spot the Writing on the Wall

One day in early 2012, Jordi and I looked at the company's revenues and realized that we were on track to do $5 million for the year. At that point, I decided to take some of those meetings that VCs had been wanting to have—it was time to get serious about this. We raised a $5 million Series A round and I left *Wired* to become CEO of 3D Robotics in December 2012. The next year was spent evolving the company from one selling bags of parts for hobbyists to one making and selling fully autonomous GPS-guided drones, ready to fly, in a box for less than $1,000.

Step Six: Shoot for the Moon

By mid-2013, it was clear that personal, civilian, and commercial drones were hot; not only were we and others selling tens or hundreds of thousands of them, but industries from agriculture to Hollywood were waking up to the realization that drones could transform their own businesses. While traditional aerospace

(*Continued*)

(*Continued*)

companies, which had been selling high-priced drones to the military, were hit by defense cutbacks, new companies such as ours revealed that the low-cost consumer and civilian markets were potentially much larger—the PC to the aerospace industry's mainframes, as it were. The only question was which company could grow and evolve the technology fast enough to dominate this new market. Hundreds of startups entered the space, and our competitors ranged from huge French consumer electronics companies (Parrot) to a new breed of world-class Chinese companies (DJI) innovating at smartphone speed.

We had to grow even faster, so we raised another $31 million in a Series B round and started building a twenty-first-century aerospace company, shooting for Google-grade software, Apple-grade hardware, and Foxconn-grade manufacturing . . . all while still balancing the demands of an open-source community with a for-profit company.

Sounds hard? It is—but it's also incredibly exciting. We feel like we're inventing the future. Today, we're more than 300 employees, from our Tijuana drone factory, our San Diego engineering center, our Berkeley HQ, and software team, not to mention the hundreds of open-source developers around the world. This feels like the birth of a new industry, and whatever we're building it won't be anything like the aerospace companies of the past.

Step Seven: ???[14]

Step Eight: Profit!

Investor's Perspective: 3D Robotics
By Jon Callaghan (True Ventures)

In venture capital investing, sometimes you know it when you see it.

I had known Chris Anderson for a few years when he emailed me to tell me he had a crazy idea to talk with me about. Chris and I had talked a lot about hardware over the prior few years, and he was always the most advanced thinker on the state of the sensor economy. As Chris' book *Makers* was being written, he gave me great counsel on True's investments in Fitbit, MakerBot, Tinkercad, littleBits, and others. Chris was immersed in the robotics and hardware revolution from the beginning, so when he called me to discuss his "project that might need some funding," I cleared the decks and met him within a day or two. In my conference room in Palo Alto, Chris casually talked me through his creation of one of the most advanced commercial drone technology companies in the world.

The story was remarkable: GeekDad blog author tries to impress his kids with RC planes and starts hacking them with Lego Mindstorms. Turns to the Internet to collaborate on ideas, founds an open-source movement behind DIY drones, meets co-founder over email, and builds a factory. Movement takes off in all directions. A company is born.

As we talked, my mind exploded with the enormous market possibilities enabled by low-cost, autonomous flying vehicles. As a pilot, I immediately understood the capabilities and power that come with autopilot control, and I had witnessed how Moore's Law changed the face of commercial and general aviation in incredible ways over the past few years. As smartphones proliferated, all component costs were dropping rapidly, and the vision of a combination of robotics, low-cost components, and autopilot software was an easy one for me to see. As we sat in Palo Alto discussing possible applications for autonomous flight, Chris turned to me and said, "As for applications, I'm not really sure. After all, what did you need a personal computer for when they first came out?"

The investment decision in 3D Robotics was straightforward in my view: Here, I had one of the best thinkers and visionaries in technology, who had built a company from his kitchen table to $5 million in revenues in less than two years. Not only had he done this on zero dollars, but he assembled a team and started a movement. He was building and shipping products globally, and he was at the forefront of one of the biggest potential markets of our time.

Our mission at True is to invest behind great people in great markets. It's that simple. Invest behind the smartest creative founders and work hard to be extremely early in very large potential markets. Today's creative founder is the most powerful force in our economy and society. They see the future before we do, and they push ahead to build it, fearless of the obstacles that are sure to challenge them. I believe that venture capital should be at the forefront of solving the biggest problems of our society, pushing the bounds of the biggest and most promising technologies, and moving our understanding of science and our world forward. What we should be about is risk maximization: Take the biggest risks possible in certain ways (product, market, timing), but limit risk by working with incredibly gifted founders developing core technology in a capital-efficient manner.

I have made a career and built an entire firm around these beliefs, so imagine how exciting it was to meet Chris, hear his story about starting 3D Robotics, and see the future through his eyes.

True committed to lead very, very quickly.

With Chris Anderson and 3D Robotics, we knew it when we saw it.

Notes

1. Jeffrey A. Timmons and Stephen Spinelli, *New Venture Creation: Entrepreneurship for the 21st Century* (New York: McGraw Hill International, 2010).
2. David Cohen and Brad Feld, *Do More Faster* (Hoboken, NJ: John Wiley & Sons, 2011), 227–229.
3. Mark Suster, "Invest in Lines, Not Dots," *Both Sides of the Table*, November 15, 2010, www.bothsidesofthetable.com/2010/11/15/invest-in-lines-not-dots/.

4. *Dragons' Den*: Season 4, Episode 8.
5. *Dragons' Den*: Season 4, Episode 6.
6. Douglas R. Hofstadter, *Gödel, Escher, Bach: An Eternal Golden Braid* (New York: Basic Books, 1979).
7. William J. Cameron's "Chapter 5: Find the Money to Finance Your Project" from William R. Cobb, *Business Alchemy: Turning Ideas into Gold* (Bloomington, IN: AuthorHouse, 2012).
8. Tony Bailetti and Sonia D. Bot, "An Ecosystem-Based Job-Creation Engine Fueled by Technology Entrepreneurs," *Technology Innovation Management Review*, February 2013, http://timreview.ca/article/658.
9. See Brad's book *Startup Communities: Building an Entrepreneurial Ecosystem in Your City* for a detailed discussion around startup communities.
10. Union Square Ventures Investment Thesis, https://www.usv.com/posts/investment-thesis-usv.
11. Bessemer Venture Partners Anti-Portfolio is a refreshing counter-example: http://www.bvp.com/portfolio/antiportfolio.
12. Brad Feld, "Saying No in Less Than 60 Seconds," Brad Feld blog, June 28, 2009, http://www.feld.com/archives/2009/06/say-no-in-less-than-60-seconds.html.
13. *Dragons' Den*: Season 3, Episode 1.
14. This wonderful reference comes from the South Park underpants gnomes guide to business, seen at http://southpark.cc.com/clips/151008/ underpants-gnomes.

12

CHAPTER

Pitfalls

Even after hearing tens of thousands of pitches, there are some statements that still turn our stomachs. Some of these issues show a lack of business acumen, others illustrate the dark side of the optimism of entrepreneurship, and some simply make the founders look naïve. As we wrap up our discussion about startup opportunities, we explore various pitfalls that undermine an investor's confidence in a company. As an entrepreneur, think hard about whether you are falling into one of these traps when describing your new company.

Showstoppers and Red Herrings

Showstoppers are major obstacles facing the entrepreneur. They can also be statements that you might make about your business or market that would give an investor doubts about how well you understand your business, and therefore, your likelihood of success. They include:

- The market is wrong.
- We haven't found our customers yet.
- We don't own the solution.
- Making money isn't our primary goal.
- Large Company X (e.g., Google, Ford, AT&T) just doesn't get it.
- We have no revenue model.

A red herring refers to a distraction that diverts attention from more important issues. In evaluating a new business, these are some statements that cause an investor to think that the entrepreneur doesn't have a clue. Here are few of our favorites:

- "We have no competition."
- "Our financials are conservative."
- "If we get only 2 percent of the market . . ."

When entrepreneurs make such statements, investors interpret them as:

- "We have no competition." Either you don't know how to use Google or your idea is a bad one.
- "Our financials are conservative." How can they be? In most cases, financial projections are wrong and are not based on experience.
- "If we get only 2 percent of the market . . ." Regardless of the size of your market, 2 percent is a big percentage for a brand-new entrant.

Entrepreneurs need investors more than investors need entrepreneurs. Thus, the best investors have many opportunities to review, and they are always on the lookout for a reason to say no. Be wary of including showstoppers or red herrings in your presentation as they give investors an easy way out.

Excessive Valuation

A primary reason deals fail to materialize on *Dragons' Den* and *Shark Tank* is valuation. In many cases, the entrepreneurs are asking for too much money for too little equity. When you are at the very beginning of your company's journey, seeking $500,000 for 5 percent of your company is unreasonable and often insulting to experienced angel investors.

The decision to make an investment is the first step in a negotiation process. Once an investor decides to make an investment, she then must come to an agreement with the entrepreneur on terms both are happy with. The terms are more complicated and fluid and depend on a number of factors, including how badly the investor wants to invest, how much the entrepreneur needs the investment, what other options the entrepreneur has, and whether the entrepreneur and investor can bridge the gap between what each thinks is reasonable.

While it's the investor's responsibility to make an offer, a savvy investor will often ask an entrepreneur what valuation they are expecting. Recognize that this is often a test—the investor isn't yet negotiating, but is trying to decide if the entrepreneur has a reasonable set of expectations. How the entrepreneur answers this question is much more important than the actual answer. Investors want to see if you have the business acumen to value your company appropriately given its stage and progress to date. If the investor thinks you are unrealistic or irrational, even if the investor has interest in investing, he will often disengage at this point.

SwimZip[1] founders Betsy Johnson and Berry Wanless were seeking $60,000 for 5 percent of their bathing suit business that features a signature full-length zipper down the front that makes the suit extremely easy to put on and take off. Additionally, both the tops and bottoms block 98 percent of UVA and UVB cancer-causing rays. But was it worth a valuation of $1.2 million at this stage? Kevin O'Leary certainly didn't think so. He believed their valuation was closer to $500,000. Lori Greiner believed SwimZip to be worth even less and offered $60,000 at a $300,000 valuation. After much discussion, the swimsuit founders accepted Lori's offer, giving up 20 percent of their company and securing a deal with her.

Don't fall into the excessive valuation trap. Remember, you don't have to be right, just reasonable.

Taboo Businesses

Some industries are nonstarters. Pornography, drugs, gambling, and other illicit activities are taboo to many investors and will encounter difficulty in garnering support even though they may be lucrative. Even secondary services to these industries, such as digital secure payments for online casinos, may be shunned by investors.

Kevin O'Leary once commented that, while he himself didn't have issues with innovations based in taboo fields, he still wouldn't support them. His reasoning was based on an inverse halo effect. Kevin felt that if he endorsed a taboo product, even through a passive investment, it might negatively impact his other investments.

Taboos tend to be binary. There is very little middle ground.

No Skin in the Game

Investors like to see entrepreneurs have skin in the game. After all, if the founders don't have their money invested and at risk, why should an investor? It is worth noting that the amount of capital required for having skin in the game will vary. For an entrepreneur still in college, a maxed-out credit card would be considered enough. For a seasoned serial entrepreneur, it would take significantly more.

For their company Veggie Mama,[2] Theresa and Robert Fraijo had huge amounts of sweat equity in their venture. Robert had dropped out of law school to start the business and Theresa sold the diamond out of her engagement ring. The couple borrowed money from friends and family and moved into Robert's parents' house. Investors Robert Herjavec and Lori Greiner saw, from these actions, that the couple had the determination to bring their veggie pops to market. Thus, Veggie Mama was born with the $150,000 investment and a $750,000 post-money valuation.

Rest assured, no one requires you to sell your car or mortgage your home, although these are powerful signals of your commitment.

The No Asshole Rule

Creating disruptive innovation is difficult. Getting it widely adopted in the marketplace is almost impossible. Regardless of the product, service, or solution, one thing remains true—it is hard work. Innovators continuously struggle to overcome product hurdles, economic scarcity, and technological barriers. For that reason, many investors have adopted a No Asshole Rule.[3]

Bringing innovation to the market is hard enough without having to deal with assholes. Most investors stay close to the company for many years, talking weekly, if not daily, to the founders they have backed. Investors want to ensure that the only source of stress comes from external forces, not internal egos.

We are not suggesting that if the entrepreneur is nice, everything will be great. Instead, we operate from the truism that "Life is too short." The more friction an entrepreneur establishes in the early interactions with an investor, the less the investor will be interested in working with the entrepreneur.

The Key Person Dependency

As an entrepreneur, you should be collecting the best talent you possibly can, including other co-founders, investors, advisors, and early employees. Single-founder businesses are subject to a risk often referred to as a key person dependency, where the individual founder is vital not only to the innovation strategy but is also critical to the delivery process.

Kevin O'Leary is famous for asking innovators: "So what happens if you get hit by a bus tomorrow? Does the business also die?" What O'Leary is exploring is the key person dependency issue. No one wants to fund an opportunity where the entire business is dependent on one person.

Scalability requires the innovation to be replicable. If a key person is needed to replicate the value added to the customer each time, then the business' growth will be gated by the capacity of that key founder. Work hard to eliminate this dependency from the very beginning by recruiting and adding amazing people to your team.

Drinking Your Own Kool-Aid

An echo chamber is a hollow space that produces reverberating sound. While it may be good for acoustic manipulation, it is not good for innovation. An entrepreneur who only seeks and listens to feedback that agrees with her position is said to be living in an echo chamber. Investors also refer to founders who willfully blind themselves to potential issues with their business as "drinking their own Kool-Aid."[4]

An innovator who only discusses the opportunity or solution with those in the inner circle falls prey to the downside of drinking his own Kool-Aid. By only listening to those who agree with you, it is likely your judgments will be biased. Many founders want to hide their innovations from the world, afraid they could be stolen. But keeping your innovation a secret and not getting critical feedback early and often is a recipe for disaster.

An essential component of the Lean Startup movement is getting critical feedback for your idea on a continual basis. That is why so many innovators in the Lean Startup movement push for sharing ideas early and often. If the only people who have told you your idea is awesome are related to you, you may have a problem.

During season one of *Dragons' Den*, a hardworking entrepreneur was pitching a leather armchair that converted to an all-in-one exercise unit. It sounded like a horrible idea, but the entrepreneur was passionate about it. When asked why he was so enthusiastic, the founder said, "Everyone I show this to says this is a great idea. They tell me it is a great product." When the investors asked the entrepreneur who these people were, he confessed that all feedback was from close friends and family members. Without an unbiased view, especially from potential customers, this founder was demonstrating the dangers of the echo chamber.

Founder's Perspective: Zenie Bottle
By Paul Berberian (Founder)

Memories lie.

I remember myself as a much better businessperson. In third grade, I had my first business. I sold Genie Bottles. I got the formula from my cousin. Think snow globe, but instead of falling flakes when you shake the globe, I made a bottle filled with magic goo. When the bottle was shaken, the clear, colored liquid transformed into an opaque, iridescent storm that's as mesmerizing as a lava lamp. I made 40 bottles, took them to school and sold them for 25 cents. I sold out in minutes. (I made a cool $10—not adjusted for inflation.) Every kid at May-field Elementary wanted a Genie Bottle. The next day, I doubled my price and doubled my production run. Kids were lining up to buy Genie Bottles before I got to school and I just knew I was going to be rich!

A struggle broke out, a bottle fell, glass broke, and kids cried. I was summoned to Sister Sheila's office and my parents were called. My Genie Bottle days were over.

Fast-forward 32 years, and my daughter needed to create a product to sell at her "mini-society" market, a one-day fair where kids make items and then barter to learn about commerce. My kid was going to dominate—no friendship bracelets or fuzzy pencil erasers for her. She was going to make and sell Genie Bottles. Man, she cleaned up. She sold out in 15 minutes. My wife kept one special bottle as a memento of my daughter's triumphant day of business. It sat on the kitchen window sill for three years until I needed a business idea and she handed me the bottle and said sell this.

So, I did. Zenie Bottle was born because Genie Bottle couldn't be trade-marked. I had come off creating a couple of successful companies and I was feeling invincible. I convinced my brother-in-law to join me as my partner and together we raised $1 million from our friends and family. Within 12 months it failed. Here is why.

We made the product more than it was. It was nothing more than a cool novelty item. I felt novelties were beneath me. I was a tech CEO after all, and my ego needed a bigger idea. So, I made it a photo sharing, virtual keepsake, mystery bottle with a web series backstory about the magical Zenie Bottle from the land of the Yeti. It was complex. We spent a small fortune on making all the things to support this concept, and thus, the bottle became an afterthought.

We were certain a market existed for the product because I saw it go crazy twice in my life. But we never sold that product. Instead we sold the crazy idea I concocted, which turned out to be too hard to explain.

We made it out of glass, but tried to sell it to kids. Moms don't like hand-blown glass bottles with a nasty fluid paired with instructions for the child to shake it violently.

We scaled the business hoping for success and made a lot of bottles, but they never sold.

I believed in my heart it would sell. I had such a strong emotional tie to the idea. Thankfully, my partner did not. After we spent about $650,000, we met one Saturday afternoon to discuss the business and he declared it dead. Several months of promoting resulted in only a handful of legitimate sales. I resisted, but the numbers didn't lie. Only my memories deceived me. The following Monday, we shut down the business.

Investor's Perspective: Zenie Bottle
By Brad Feld (Investor)

Paul Berberian is an awesome entrepreneur. I was a seed investor in his second company, Raindance Communications, which ended up going public, surviving the crash of the Internet bubble, and, ultimately, being acquired by West. Paul was a classic tech/Internet entrepreneur, which is whom I invest in, so when he called me and told me he wanted to talk about his new company, I was excited.

After a few minutes of listening to the Genie Bottle/Zenie Bottle conception story, I silently thought, "What the fuck is Paul doing? This is silly." But I kept listening because I had become close friends with Paul, had been successful investing in his last company, and wanted to be supportive of wherever his entrepreneurial passions took him.

At the end of the conversation, he said he was raising $1 million and asked if I'd invest. Even though I wasn't very interested in the Zenie Bottle and was skeptical that it would turn into anything, I wanted to be helpful to Paul so I invested $25,000, which was a typical angel investment for me at the time. Basically, I invested because of Paul, not because of the idea.

Over the next six months, whenever Paul and I would get together, he'd share his ever-expanding vision for the Zenie Bottle. It felt off to me, but I didn't

(Continued)

(*Continued*)

feel like I had instincts for the business, so I was supportive, but expressed my concerns as clearly as I could.

By about nine months in, Paul had a lot of Zenie Bottles and was selling almost none of them. At this point, he started asking harder questions of himself and for the first time, stopped drinking his own Kool-Aid. He knew things weren't working and was now open to feedback on whether the opportunity was worth spending any time on.

One day, Paul called and said, "I'm done with Zenie Bottle—I'm shutting it down." We went out for a meal and had a good talk, and I gave him a big hug. He failed gracefully, selling off some of the software and recovering some money for his investors.

Several years later, I invested in the seed round of Sphero, a new company that Paul co-founded that had gone through Techstars. Today, Sphero is a 175-plus person company with several very popular consumer products, including Sphero, Ollie, and BB-8. It turns out that kids, and their parents, are a lot more interested in cool robot toys than they are in weird bong-like bottles filled with scary liquid. Paul learned a lot from the Zenie Bottle experience, and I'm glad to be on another entrepreneurial ride with him.

Notes

1. *Shark Tank*: Season 5, Episode 15.
2. *Shark Tank*: Season 5, Episode 5.
3. The No Asshole Rule is different from the 3-Asses Rule coined by software investor Jeff Clavier of SoftTech VC. In order for a startup to be an opportunity for Jeff to be interested in it must have: (1) a smart-ass team, (2) a kick-ass product, and (3) a big-ass market.
4. We recognize this particular cliché is an insensitive one because of the tragedy at Jonestown. But, like many contemporary clichés, it lives on.

13

Don't Quit Your Day Job If You Aren't . . .

Passionate about the Space

Being an entrepreneur is an extremely difficult job. It can be lonely, full of uncertainty, and often requires huge sacrifice. Most people need to be in love (*love*, not like) with their startup to completely dedicate themselves to it. If you aren't passionate about your solution, how could your customers be?

Able to Execute the Solution

Ideas are nice, but execution builds value. If you aren't confident that you can not only build the solution, but also bring it to market, don't quit your day job (at least until you bring on a co-founder who can).

Certain That the Problem Is a Need (as Opposed to a Want)

New product adoption is difficult. If your solution does not solve a compelling unmet need, it is unlikely that you'll get traction. Build solutions that are aspirin not vitamins. Find services that have inelastic demand. Don't quit your day job if your solution is only a nice to have instead of a must have.

Certain That the Problem Is Shared by a Large (and Growing) Market

A rising tide lifts all boats. If your startup does not sell into a market that is growing year over year, and will continue to do so for the foreseeable future, don't quit your day job.

Able to Offer a Solution That Is 10× Better Than Anything Else in the Market

To displace incumbents, startup solutions must be exponentially better (not incrementally). If they aren't, it is unlikely that you will be able to overcome the lead and momentum market leaders have. Customers won't abandon sunk costs and accepted realities for something that is just a little better. Don't quit your day job until you have a solution that is 10× faster, cheaper, more secure, or bigger.

Ready to "Burn the Ships"

Explorers often burned their ships to signal to their crew that there was no going home. Are you ready to make the same level of commitment? If not, then don't quit your day job.

Able to Access Potential Customers

Today, customer-centric innovation is the focus. You need to test your product by getting it in front of actual customers. If you are limited in your ability to do this, then don't quit your day job.

Able to Spend Six Months without Personal Income

In our always on, 24/7, global economy, it takes time to develop a solution, test the market, and prepare to scale. If you can't afford to wait for revenue, then don't quit your day job.

Able to Garner Enough People, Users, and Money to Create a Minimum Viable Product

Testing requires an MVP. If you can't create such a product (even a paper-based version), then don't quit your day job.

Prepared to Get into the Weeds and Do the Grunt Work

You are your startup. There are no shortcuts. Even overnight successes take lots of hard work and continuous focus. If you aren't committed to doing everything and anything needed, then don't quit your day job.

Glossary

800-pound gorilla: A marketing term for the largest player in a market, one that is so dominant it can do whatever it wants without regard to the competition. For example, Amazon.com is the 800-pound gorilla in the book industry.

10× Rule: To displace incumbents, a new solution must be exponentially better, faster, cheaper, stronger, etc. Being a little better isn't enough. For example, e-mail was so widely adopted because it was 10× faster than the traditional postal service.

arm's length: A term of law, referring to two parties not otherwise connected. If you sell property to a family member, there may be concern that the transaction was not at "arm's length" and the property might have been sold for less than it is worth. As another example, a buyer may request an "arm's length audit" of a company's financials before buying.

ARPU: A retail term, average revenue per user, referring to how much money each user will generate for the solution provider. For example, on average, each new user of iTunes buys $100 worth of music in her first year. Thus, the ARPU for iTunes would be $100.

availability bias: Our thinking is greatly influenced by what is personally relevant, impactful, and recent. We estimate the probability of an outcome based on how easy that outcome is to imagine.

back channels: A business term referring to an alternative secondary and less formal communication stream. For example, once negotiations broke down formally, the assistants had to resort to back channels to obtain the food order for dinner.

barrier to entry: An economics term referring to a cost or hindrance that must be overcome before advancement. For example, obtaining a taxi license is a barrier to entry for most drivers.

beachhead: A military term referring to a landing area first secured before the advancement of troops. Facebook's beachhead was U.S. universities. In its first few years, only currently enrolled students at U.S. colleges could access the service.

break-even point: An accounting term referring to the moment in time when revenue equals expenses. For example, after six months of great sales, the startup was at the break-even point.

business acumen: Skills and experience in the development of strategy and the execution of business planning. For example, the new CEO had run similar-size companies before. He had a lot of business acumen to share.

CAGR: An accounting term, compound annual growth rate, representing how fast an industry is growing year after year.

CoCA: An accounting term, cost of client acquisition, representing how much must be spent to attract one more customer. For example, the website spent $1,000,000 on advertising, but 100,000 new users signed up. That pegs the CoCA at $10/user.

competition, bad: An axiom representing business rivals that threaten your business.

competition, good: An axiom representing business rivals that make your business look good.

confirmation bias: The tendency to favor external information that confirms your preconceptions and to dismiss negative feedback.

creative destruction: A business term referring to the process by which disruptive technologies lead to massive market change. The new idea leads to the creative destruction of the old idea; for example, cars disrupted the horse-drawn carriage industry.

disruptive innovation: A technology that radically changes the market on entry, typically generated only when the 10× Rule is in play.

domain knowledge: Understanding the customers and the industry in your business domain.

double dipping: An entrepreneurial axiom referring to an activity that generates multiple benefits and revenue streams. For example,

George Lucas double dipped when he began to produce licensed *Star Wars* merchandise, thus generating many revenue streams from the movie (at the box office, from the DVD, and from other branded merchandise).

due diligence: A legal term for the process by which transactional material information is confirmed. For example, typically before a company is acquired, due diligence will be conducted to ensure all patents are properly filed.

economy of scale: An economics concept that describes how a venture gains cost advantages from expanding sales. For example, as the shoemaker sold more sandals, he could buy material in bulk. This economy of scale leads to cost savings that give the shoemaker the ability to lower his prices.

elasticity of demand: An economic theory that posits that price impacts the consumption of some products. For example, the demand for water is inelastic because, if scarce, people will pay any price for it. The price of goldfish is elastic because demand varies with trends in pet ownership, and goldfish are not essential goods.

elevator pitch: A short verbal proposal used by an entrepreneur to illustrate the key points of an opportunity.

escalating commitment: A psychological term that denotes a decision maker's increased reinvestment of resources in a losing course of action. This bias is often caused by our desire to not accept loss. For example, the investor wasn't prepared to write off his investment in startup X; instead, he put good money after bad as part of his escalating commitment to this deal.

exit: An investment term referring to a point in time when investors can liquidate their investment and claim their profits. For example, when Facebook eventually goes public, the exit for many will be worth millions.

gating items: A decision-making term referring to an action that must occur before continuation. For example, the investor made the assignment of intellectual property a gating item to funding.

guerrilla marketing: A term for nontraditional promotional marketing that relies on time, energy, and bandwidth instead of big budgets. For example, the startup hired a chalk artist to draw graffiti on the sidewalk in front of its customers' offices as a form of guerilla marketing.

halo effect: A marketing term for the goodwill you generate through positive association with a well-known brand or person. For example, when

Bill Gates joined the board of startup XY, his halo effect led to funding as investors' confidence grew.

intellectual property: A legal term for patents, copyright, and trademarks. For example, the company had more than 100 patents as part of its strong intellectual property portfolio.

known/in the know: To be known is to have name recognition in an industry. To be in the know is to understand that industry and who the key players are.

magic risk: The risk associated with product development. For example, if it is not 10× better than all other options, the magic risk will be too large.

management risk: The risk associated with leadership. For example, having never run a startup before, the team had lots of management risk.

market risk: The risk associated with market adoption. For example, since your product must go on sale, you don't know what the demand will be, so you have high market risk.

minimal viable product (MVP):   A startup term for the least feature-rich product you can show your potential users, customers, and clients. Often labeled "beta." For example, the MVP for an email platform is the ability to securely and reliably transfer text from one person to another.

next value inflection point: An investment term referring to the subsequent future milestone that will lead to an increase in the overall value of the venture. For example, once they began selling the app, they hit a next value inflection point since market risk was mitigated.

operational experience: Refers to founders' prior know-how about the building and delivery of the solution. For example, as the startup was producing apps for the iPhone, additional operational experience in mobile software was recruited.

opportunity cost: The cost of the best option or alternative taken. It encompasses all the sacrifices needed to be made to pursue a plan of action. For example, in quitting a job to pursue an MBA, the opportunity cost includes lost wages.

pain point: The problem your solution addresses. For example, one of the pain points email solved was the slowness of the postal service.

personal attribution error: An internal bias that leads you to blame others for their mistakes, but you blame your own mistakes on circumstances.

piggybacking: A marketing term in which a new product enters the market by leveraging an existing product's brand loyalty. For example, when I purchased a bottle of vodka, the store gave me a sample of a new cocktail mix, effectively piggybacking on my vodka purchase.

planning fallacy: A psychological term for the tendency you have to underestimate the time or work needed to complete tasks.

premature scaling: An entrepreneurial term representing the risk of growing the venture before it is appropriate. Pets.com failed because it scaled prematurely. Before it even sold a dollar's worth of product, the founders had invested millions in inventory.

proof of concept: Originally a term referring to a prototype proving a technical solution's feasibility. Recently, the term has become synonymous with early-stage revenue-proving market feasibility. For example, without proof of concept revenue for early adopters, the inventor was having difficulty proving anyone needed what he had built.

prospect theory: A psychological term for the decision-making process in which risk probabilities are known and used to influence the decision.

red flag: A naval term for a danger warning. For example, the sale of the startup failed when criminal records were found on each founder. The investor couldn't get past that red flag.

red herring: Something that distracts from the more important issue at hand. In the case of a business, it is often used to refer to an entrepreneur's fixation on a concept or metric that she thinks is important, but is not.

revenue model: A business term referring to the method a venture will use to generate sales, monetize assets, and sustain itself.

Rogers' Diffusion of Innovations Theory: A theory that attempts to explain how, why, and at what rate new solutions roll out across society.

scale/scalability: An economic term referring to the ability to increase sales without commensurately increasing costs.

serial entrepreneur: A business term for an entrepreneur who has successfully exited more than one company.

signaling theory: A term for the influence that one party credibly conveys to another party by its action. Like the halo effect. For example, when Bill Gates funded startup XY, it sent a signal to other investors.

skin in the game: A phrase representing what founders have at stake in the startup. If a founder is only working on his startup on the side, he may not have enough skin in the game to satisfy an investor.

suboptimal solutions: A solution that does not fully meet the needs of the end users. In addressing these unmet needs, startups are disruptive technologies.

sweat equity: A term used to describe an ownership interest in a company that was procured by hard work and not by a direct financial investment. Usually associated with founders. For example, for the last year, Founder Y has not received a salary. He considers the opportunity cost his sweat equity.

talent triangle: A business concept used to explain and qualify a startup management team.

third-party validation: Arm's-length evidence of your success. For example, sales are the best third-party validation because they mitigate market risk.

total addressable market: The subset of all possible customers for your solution.

traction: A form of proof of concept and third-party validation; this term refers to acceptance in the market from end uses. For example, the app startup acquired traction after its app was downloaded more than 10,000 times in one day.

valuation, postmoney: What a company is worth the moment after funding, calculated as the premoney valuation plus the cash invested.

valuation, premoney: What a company is worth the moment before funding.

viral marketing: A form of guerrilla marketing in which each person touched by the marketing passes it along to at least two other people. For example, the video became viral the moment people started forwarding it to all their friends.

willful blindness: A legal term for choosing to ignore a key negative factor to avoid liability, often used colloquially in entrepreneurship for simply choosing to ignore something negative to avoid confronting it.

Acknowledgments

In 2014, during a conversation we were having about Sean's video series *The Naked Entrepreneur*, we started talking about doing a book together to answer the question we each get asked all the time, "Is this a good idea?"

We started chewing on the idea for *Startup Opportunities*, and Sean was ready to go. Brad had a few false starts, but Sean stayed with him, even after Brad had a moment of total overwhelm and said, "I can't deal with this right now." We finally kicked into high gear in the summer, and when Brad returned from his sabbatical in November 2014, we were both refreshed and ready to finish things off.

The first edition of this book wouldn't exist without the help of our friends at FG Press: Dane McDonald, Eugene Wan, Kevin Kane, and Dave Heal. Even though FG Press wasn't a successful venture, its team's patience, diligence, hard work, and endless professionalism was inspiring.

Wiley, with which Brad has published five other books, decided to publish a second edition of this book. We tidied it up, added a few things, and let the Wiley editing and production crew do their magic. Once again, we had the pleasure to work with Bill Falloon, who is Brad's long-time editor.

Every book is challenging to write. In this case, we've both had enormous help from many of the people we've gotten to work with, along with exposure to endless ideas for new companies, often as many as 10 a day.

For starters, we stand on the shoulders of giants in the contemporary startup revolution. Steve Blank, Eric Ries, Alex Osterwalder, and Bill Aulet have each contributed extraordinary amounts of thinking, along with key books, toward helping people understand the process of creating a startup. We have deep respect for each of them and what they've done, and hope this book can add at least a little to the current body of knowledge around starting companies.

Many entrepreneurs and investors contributed examples to the book. Thanks to Tim Ferriss, Isaac Saldana, Mark Solon, Carly Gloge, Stephanie Palmeri, Matt Galligan, Barbara Stegemann, W. Brett Wilson, Amanda Steinberg, Joanne Wilson, Jeff Lawson, Chris Sacca, Shane Talbott, Kevin O'Leary, Daniel Ha, Naval Ravikant, Alex White, Chris Anderson, Jon Callaghan, and Paul Berberian for their contributions.

Also, thanks to Steven Gedeon, Dave Valliere, and John Pinsent for their longer-form essays on complicated topics. Sean's partners and Ryerson Futures Fund also deserve some love for all their input, for their patience, and for providing such a rich environment to learn from. Thanks to Ryerson University, Canada's home for entrepreneurship education, and its faculty for all their support.

Sean has been deeply involved in *Dragons' Den* for many years. Thanks to all the participants of the show, as well as participants of its cousin, *Shark Tank*, for baring their souls, sharing their ideas, and pitching their hearts out. Also, thanks to the Dragons, Sharks, organizers, and producers of the shows for bringing the art of entrepreneurial pitching and the early-stage funding process to prime time for so many people who had never seen it before. Sometimes funny, sometimes heartbreaking, these shows are always informative and entertaining.

Brad has learned an incredible amount from Steve Case, Scott Case, and Marc Nager through his involvement in Startup America, the Startup America Partnership, Startup Weekend, and UP Global. Thanks, guys, for letting Brad be part of the team.

David Cohen, the co-founder of Techstars, has contributed in so many ways, well beyond the several sidebars he wrote for this book. David, thanks for everything you do for entrepreneurs around the world and for continuing to inspire us.

Brad's partners at Foundry Group are calm listeners to all of Brad's bitching and crankiness when he's deep in the writing process. Their support for books like this, and their effort to spread joy, love, and education to entrepreneurs everywhere is a core value that plays out daily at Foundry Group. Without them, it's likely Brad would move to Homer, Alaska, and live out his days reading science fiction with his wife, Amy Batchelor. Guys, thanks for everything. And, as a special bonus, thanks, Jason, for writing your side of the Next Big Sound example.

Finally, nothing would happen in Brad's world without the support of his wife, Amy. Her endless encouragement of his writing, her willingness to drop what she's doing and spend a day editing whatever the latest draft is, and her continuous cheerleading in the face of an onslaught of things that take Brad away from time with her is treasured.

And while on the subject of family, Sean's best investment came in marrying his wife, Marisa. During the writing of this book, somewhere between first draft and final manuscript, that investment paid a healthy dividend in the form of their son, Edison Atlas Wise. Thank you to both Marisa and Edison (the Boy Wonder) for reminding Sean what truly matters.

About the Authors

Brad Feld has been an early-stage investor and entrepreneur for over 30 years. He lives in Boulder, Colorado, and Homer, Alaska, with his wife, Amy.

Prior to co-founding Foundry Group, he co-founded Mobius Venture Capital, and prior to that, founded Intensity Ventures. Brad is also a co-founder of Techstars.

In addition to his investing efforts, Brad has been active with several nonprofit organizations. He currently is chair of the National Center for Women & Information Technology and on the boards of Path Forward, the Kauffman Fellows, and Defy Ventures.

Brad is a writer and speaker on the topics of venture capital investing and entrepreneurship. He's written a number of books as part of the Startup Revolution series and writes the blogs *Feld Thoughts* and *Venture Deals*.

Brad holds Bachelor of Science and Master of Science degrees in Management Science from the Massachusetts Institute of Technology. Brad is also an art collector and long-distance runner. He has completed 24 marathons as part of his mission to finish a marathon in each of the 50 states.

Sean Wise, PhD, is an expert on startups and venture capital. He uses this expertise in his various roles as university professor, best-selling author, international business speaker, and partner at Ryerson Futures, a seed-stage venture capital fund and technology accelerator.

Sean has published five books and more than two dozen peer-reviewed research papers and case studies of high-growth startups.

Sean spent five seasons as a consultant for CBC on the megahit venture reality show *Dragons' Den* before moving in front of the camera as the host of *The Naked Entrepreneur,* which airs on the Oprah Winfrey Network.

Sean has been called the Dr. Phil of Entrepreneurship, and in 2014, he was named Entrepreneurial Mentor of the Year by Startup Canada.

Index

READ ON FOR AN EXCERPT FROM
BRAD FELD'S

VENTURE DEALS,
THIRD EDITION

Crowdfunding

When we wrote the first version of this book in 2011, the idea of using crowdfunding as a financing mechanism was nascent. Since then, it has emerged as a powerful approach, both for product development and equity financing. In this chapter we will discuss the various crowdfunding approaches and legal implications, and how crowdfunding differs from more traditional methods.

Product Crowdfunding

Crowdfunding typically refers to two different approaches that are relevant to financing companies. The first, popularized by Kickstarter and Indiegogo, is *product crowdfunding*.

Product crowdfunding is typically used for physical products. The company puts its product idea up on Kickstarter along with content showing what the product will do and a series of different rewards for backers. In most cases, the product is in an early design stage and far from ready to ship. The rewards vary by dollar amount and often include things that, while linked to the product, are experiential or tangential to the product, such as logoed stickers and T-shirts, sponsorship recognition, or real-world events to celebrate the launch of the product.

Most campaigns have a 30-day funding target that, if not achieved, results in the campaign failing and funding not occurring. This is the hardware equivalent of building a software *minimum viable product (MVP)*. If the campaign is successful, you know you have a compelling MVP. If the campaign does not reach its funding target, your potential customers are telling you that your MVP is not interesting enough to pursue.

Several high profile products got their start on Kickstarter, including the Pebble Watch (which raised $10.2 million in 30 days) and Oculus Rift (which raised $2.5 million in 30 days). Companies have also had similar successes on Indiegogo, such as TrackR, which raised $1.7 million.

If this sounds similar to a preorder campaign, it is, and you will also hear people refer to them as "presales" or "preorders." While Kickstarter, Indiegogo, and other crowdfunding sites are growing rapidly, some companies, such as Glowforge, have decided to run their own preorder campaigns. In Glowforge's case, they raised $27.9 million in 30 days, demonstrating that if you have a compelling product and are sophisticated around marketing and promoting your product, you can run a very successful preorder campaign on your own.

The crowdfunding approach can even be rolled into your business model. When we invested in Betabrand, they were building a two-sided clothing marketplace that incorporated the notion of crowdfunding into their design process. Individual designers can create new designs that are then promoted on Betabrand's website. Customers preorder the designs and if a certain preorder threshold is met, the design is produced and becomes a permanent product in Betabrand's catalog.

In each of these cases, one of the large advantages of this approach is that the funding is nondilutive as no equity is involved. Instead of selling equity or debt, you are preselling a product and collecting the cash up front.

The downside of product crowdfunding is the situation where a campaign is successful but the company doesn't finish building the product. In some cases, the company is able to raise addition capital, often equity, to complete the product and fulfill the preorders. In others, the company never ships the product or only fulfills some aspect of the campaign. While this situation is disappointing, the culture around product crowdfunding is such that these failures are understood to be part of the process, in the same way that investing equity in a company does not necessarily result in a successful company and a return on the investment.

Equity Crowdfunding

The second crowdfunding approach, popularized by AngelList, is equity crowdfunding. This approach pertains to the situation when an investor gives money to a company in exchange for a security (either debt or equity) through an intermediated process, often involving an online funding platform. These platforms, such as AngelList, allow companies to essentially advertise their funding or use the power of a social network to attract other investor interest. Evolved approaches, such as AngelList Syndicates, allow individual investors to aggregate other investors to participate in their syndicate, acting like a small version of a venture capital fund.

While crowdfunding has expanded to cover many different situations, there are tight legal definitions surrounding each approach that were defined as part of the JOBS Act (the full name is the Jumpstart Our Business Startups Act) that was passed in 2012. As a result, some of the aspects of fundraising on platforms like AngelList are referred to as crowdfunding, but are really not anything new, other than the use of an online platform to connect companies with potential investors.

In the United States, if you are selling a *security*, you need to register the security with the Securities and Exchange Commission (SEC) unless you have an exemption not to. A security is any financial instrument that gives you an ownership interest in a company, including common stock, preferred stock, or convertible debt. This doesn't include revenue derived from product crowdfunding or a preorder campaign. The original rules for registering securities were defined in the Securities Act of 1933, and, while they have evolved, are still based on rules negotiated more than 80 years ago.

Fortunately, there are a number of exemptions that allow you to avoid an SEC registration. In general, unless you are taking a company public via initial public offering (IPO), you won't have to worry about registering your offering with the SEC. However, there are important guidelines that you must follow in order not to blow up your ability to rely on an exemption. The two most important to understand are the concept of an *accredited investor* and the process of *general solicitation*.

An accredited investor is a person who has a substantial net worth or income, as defined by the SEC and changed from time to time. In most cases, entities such as a VC, a corporation with meaningful assets, or a registered bank automatically qualify. An individual qualifies if she earns $200,000 per year or has a joint income with her spouse of $300,000 and this level has been earned in the previous two years and can be reasonably expected to be earned in the future. If an individual doesn't have this level of income, she can qualify if she has a net worth exceeding $1 million either alone or jointly with her spouse.

Unlike an accredited investor, the SEC does not clearly define what is considered to be general solicitation, instead leaving it open to interpretation. Historically, general solicitation referred to advertising or publicly promoting your fundraising, such as specifically making a financing ask in public at an accelerator demo day. Depending on your lawyer and how conservative you are, the line of where general solicitation is crossed is vague, but the simple test is that if you don't have a preexisting relationship with someone and encounter them through something that looks like an advertisement (which could include a mass email, rather than a one-on-one introduction), then you are likely in the general solicitation bucket.

Prior to the JOBS Act, one wanted to avoid raising money from investors who were not accredited as well as avoid general solicitation. With the JOBS Act, the rules changed somewhat.

While there are an endless number of $99 courses on how to raise money for your company using crowdfunding, our friend Brad Bernthal, a law professor at CU Boulder, created the following chart as a summary of the implications of the three major crowdfunding and financing aspects of the JOBS Act. These are known as Rule 506(b), Rule 506(c)/Title II, and Title III.

	Rule 506(b)	Rule 506(c)/Title II	Title III
Aggregate cap on amount raised?	No	No	Yes ($1 million over 12 months)
General solicitation allowed?	No	Yes	No, except via a single funding portal or broker
Who can invest?	Accredited	Accredited	Accredited and nonaccredited
Broker or intermediary required?	No	No	Yes
Regulatory burden	Light	Medium	Heavy

Prior to Title II of the JOBS Act, if you generally solicited, you had broken the law and could not raise money. Prior to Title III of the JOBS Act, it was next to impossible to raise a meaningful amount of money from nonaccredited investors.

From a legal perspective, equity crowdfunding is really only Title III, where nonaccredited investors can participate. Not surprisingly, this is also the most heavily regulated approach. A company is limited to raising $1 million over a 12-month period and it can only solicit through one online funding portal or with a broker. While nonaccredited investors can participate in a Title III financing, there are limits on the size of individual investments, which, depending on the investor's net worth, can be as little at $2,000. Finally, there is a significant burden of SEC-mandated information disclosures that can easily cost a company tens of thousands of dollars to comply with.

Even though the phrase crowdfunding gets regularly applied to financings done on AngelList and other online platforms, this is often more around marketing the platform than it is around the substance of investing. Most of the financings done on AngelList happen under the 506(b) rules, which is similar to how most VC financings have historically been done. In some cases, companies use 506(c) so they can advertise more widely on a site like AngelList, but still only accept accredited investors. In these situations, there are additional regulations to ensure their investors are, indeed, accredited.

How Equity Crowdfunding Differs

A difference between equity crowdfunding and a more traditional financing is that with crowdfunding you are often setting the terms of the deal. Most sites allow you to determine the form of security you are issuing (equity versus debt) and to set all the major terms. While this is occasionally negotiated with a lead investor, in our experience most companies do not see much pushback on the terms they propose as long as they are reasonable.

While convertible debt financings are generally straightforward, they typically include a specific cap. With equity financings, a very light preferred stock with minimal protective provisions and terms are often used. Board seats, at least as part of the crowdfunding activity, are rarely offered.

The materials you put together include a traditional executive summary and a PowerPoint presentation. When raising online, you often get opportunities to spice things up with a fancy video, specific data about your recent performance, and continuous refreshes on this background information as time passes during the financing process.

In a VC-backed fundraise, you are often getting one or more self-proclaimed experts (the VC) involved in your company in an actively engaged way, either as a mentor, coach, networker, or board member. In crowdfunding situations, you are getting a crowd. While you may have a lead investor, you will now have many small investors who may, or may not, be focused on helping your company. Their investment may be a tiny dollar amount for them and they may have many separate small investments. Consequently, the responsibility on communication and engagement will be on you as it's unlikely that many of your new investors will proactively reach out to help. While this is similar to a situation where you raise money traditionally from a bunch of individual angels, it's a common dynamic in crowdfunding deals.

We've observed some companies end up being stranded after a crowdfunding round. These companies either can't, or don't, raise enough money in the crowdfunding round and find themselves without money and with a noncommitted investor syndicate. Often, these companies are not mature enough to attract a VC financing and end up in a situation where they are too early for VCs, yet don't have meaningful support from their existing crowd of investors.

Finally, watch out for the jerks. We've seen situations where one or more members of a crowdfunded financing feel overly self-important, construct belief systems around the company that are delusional, or simply regret investing and try to exert pressure on the founders in inappropriate ways. While some angel investors forget that they are supposed to be "angels" instead of "devils," some crowdfunding participants don't appear to have subscribed to the angel notion to begin with. While some of this results from lack of sophistication of some investors in crowdfunding deals, there often is less concern about reputational constraints given the dynamics of crowdfunding as compared to angel or VC investing. A final challenge with crowdfunding platforms is that it's more difficult for the entrepreneur to do detailed diligence on the crowd, so beware of the squeaky wheel who can be a real pain in the neck.